Credit Card Marketing

THE NATIONAL RETAIL FEDERATION SERIES

The National Retail Federation Series comprises books on retail store management, for stores of all sizes and for all management responsibilities. The National Retail Federation is the world's largest retail trade association, with membership that includes the leading department, specialty, discount, mass merchandise, and independent stores, as well as 30 national and 50 state associations. NRF members represent an industry that encompasses more than 1.4 million U.S. retail establishments and employs nearly 20 million people—1 in 5 American workers. The NRF's international members operate stores in more than 50 nations.

The National Retail Federation Series includes the following books.

Credit Card Marketing

Bill Grady

John Wiley & Sons, Inc.
New York • Chichester • Brisbane • Toronto • Singapore

Copyright © 1995 by A&S Companies
Published by John Wiley & Sons, Inc.

Library of Congress Cataloging-in-Publication Data:

Grady, Bill.
    Credit card marketing / Bill Grady.
       p. cm. — (National retail federation series)
    Includes bibliographical references.
    ISBN 0-471-10662-3
    1. Credit cards—United States—Marketing. I. Title.
  II. Series.
  HG3756.U54G7 1995
  332.7′85′0688—dc20   94-31487
                                          CIP

Printed in the United States of America

10 9 8 7 6 5 4 3 2 1

Wildwood Park Detective Club:
    25,15,21 8,1,22,5 10,21,19,20 2,5,7,21,14. 14,15,23 12,15,15,11 2.5,8,9,14,4 20.8,5
3,8,9,13,14.5,25 1,20 7,18,1.14,4,13,1 7.18,1,4,25,19 8,15,21,19,5 14.5,1.18 23,8,5.18,5 25,15,21
6,15,21,14,4 20.8,5 12,1,19,20, 3.12,21,5.

This book is dedicated to my children
David Grady, LaMista Aletras, Anthony Grady, and
Scott Grady, deceased—who is in our hearts forever.

ACKNOWLEDGMENTS

I would like to thank all those business associates and true friends who have made this book possible.

Special thanks to those who helped with the research and reviewed the book in progress: Sharon Brown, Dave Abright, Ross Housley, Doug Rose, and Hadley Pihl.

Thanks to those who helped with the proofing: Ashley Thigpen, Michelle Riggins, Jack Thayer, Cynthia Williams, Bill Davis, Susanne Moore, Jim Summers, Bob Klein, Jim Ballard, Paul Bedell, David Mattos, Libby Groner, Gail Taylor, Mike Burgess, and Richard Corby.

A special thank you for those who were on the team over the years: Ray Rawley, Greg Price, Ben Barone, Reggie Woodford, Cathy Brown, Larry Ward, Jeff Glazer, Bill Bonneau, Bill Taylor, Alan Sfikas, David Brendle, Vince Milam, and Beth Walters.

FOREWORD

Although millions of innovations are being made in credit marketing, several basic principles never change. This book provides a firm foundation in the basics, while giving insights into the possibilities.

Who Should Read This Book?

- Marketing managers—as a primer in the do's and don'ts of credit marketing.
- Marketing experts—as a stimulus for new ideas.
- CFOs/CEOs—as a guide for those simple penetrating questions that will keep marketing programs focused.

The credit industry is constantly changing. The pace of innovation is quickening. The variations on a theme involving airline mileage, rebates, gold cards, sweepstakes, risk/usage pricing, and so on are daunting.

Getting more for every dollar is increasingly critical. Response rates are decreasing. Targeting acquisition efforts intelligently is a key. To keep accounts active, micromanaging the portfolio based on purchase/pay patterns is a must.

This Book Tells You How!

- How to target a prescreen mailing.
- How to get prospects to take "Take Ones."
- How to get employees to want to open accounts.

- How to benefit from and avoid the pitfalls of hostess programs, premiums, telemarketing, and new resident programs.

With all the options available, with dozens of vendors suggesting how to spend precious marketing dollars, the marketing manager must analyze, plan, and show the CFO and CEO what the company is going to get for the credit marketing investment. As long as corporations look at marketing as a cost rather than a profitable investment, the marketing manager won't get all the money warranted. And the company will leave profit on the table. This book shows how to analyze, plan, and speak the CFO's language.

Bill Grady is a recognized leader in credit marketing. Many of his innovations are now standard operating procedure. You don't have to reinvent the wheel. Invest a little time and reap a huge reward!

Ralph E. Spurgin
President & CEO
Limited Credit Services, Inc.

CONTENTS

PART III
TRAINING EMPLOYEES TO MARKET CREDIT CARDS

PART IV
CREDIT CARD MARKETING TECHNIQUES

PART I

ACQUISITION PROGRAMS: BRINGING IN NEW CREDIT CARD CUSTOMERS

INTRODUCTION

Over the past 25 years, it has been my good fortune to work for and with several top retailers and financial institutions in the United States: *Lowe's Companies, Inc.,* where I introduced and managed what is today the largest retail credit card program in the home improvement center industry; *Service Merchandise,* where I introduced and managed what is now the largest retail credit card program in the catalog showroom/mass merchandising industry; and *General Electric Capital Corporation,* the largest provider of private label credit card programs in the world. I am currently associated with *Brendle's Incorporated,* as Senior Vice President, Marketing/Advertising and Store Operations, a regional discount retailer near my home town, where I played a major role in the turnaround of the company's sales and its emergence from reorganization in only 17 months. I've also worked directly or indirectly with dozens of Fortune 500 companies in their preparation of first-year marketing plans or expansion of existing credit card programs.

I wish to thank these associates—and all my many business friends over the years—for the knowledge and experience I have gained from them. This diverse background has enabled me to write the only book on credit marketing available in the credit industry. Over the years, I have initiated several firsts in this industry, including the first use of rub-offs, the mystery sale concept applied to internal employee contests, the national on-line point-of-sale instant credit program (and database), and the prepaid legal plan billed to a retail credit card program. This book is designed to be useful for both the novice and seasoned credit marketer; I hope you will find it is an invaluable reference source in your personal library. Perhaps it will be especially helpful to those who wish to pursue a career within the credit fraternity.

This book has been written in conversational form rather than in textbook fashion for two reasons: First, it should make for easier and more interesting reading, and second, that is the way I tend to speak and present programs and projects.

HISTORY

What is the function of retail, oil, or bank credit cards? Credit is like any other service (clothing alterations, free product delivery, parking facilities) offered by a retailer or bank to foster sales and revenues. Retailers and banks provide such services in the belief that the bottom line on the income statement will be better off with the service than without it. Charging customers a fee for a particular service is ultimately a pricing and marketplace decision. "Free" alterations, delivery, parking, and credit are not free to the retailer or bank providing the service. To the extent that the retailers or banks pass their costs on to the users of particular services, the added service revenues may result in lower prices for merchandise than would otherwise be the case.

Payment mechanisms such as retail credit cards, bank cards, and travel and entertainment (T&E) cards, perform two functions for consumers: satisfaction of transaction demand and satisfaction of credit demand.

In the first case, the cards satisfy customers' transaction demand for a convenient way to purchase and pay for goods. Cash, checks, travelers checks, and debit cards instantly provide for a transfer of value from the consumer to the seller, whereas retail, bank, and T&E cards provide delayed value transfer to meet the transaction demand. The seller receives payment from the issuer of the card, and in most cases, consumers may avoid finance or other charges by paying their account in full before the payment due date (these consumers are called "nonrevolvers").

In the second case, consumers use payment mechanisms to obtain credit that extends beyond the brief lag between purchase and payment. Each month, a substantial percentage of credit card users "revolve" their accounts, that is, they pay only a part of the balance owed and incur a finance charge to delay payment on the unpaid balance. The extent of this kind of use primarily reflects credit demand.

Although the payment mechanisms that retailers decide to accept obviously must accommodate consumers' transaction demand, they need not serve consumers' credit demand; a few retailers still operate on a strictly cash basis. Consumers, however, make the ultimate choice of payment mechanisms, and the development of retail and bank credit cards over the years reflects innovative adjustments to the changing needs of consumers for payment systems that meet both their transaction and credit demands.

Only 20 years ago, relatively few retailers and banks had credit card programs of their own, and consumer credit was quite small compared with payment options such as checks and cash. Today, in the 1990s, only a few retailers and banks do not have a credit card program of their own, either in-house or provided by a third party.

Consumers, in fact, now have so many credit cards to choose from that they carefully consider which bank, retail, or T&E credit cards they will carry.

BENEFITS OF CREDIT CARD PROGRAMS

As an important component of economic activity, credit cards have become a valuable tool for retailers, banks, and other financial institutions. The following list describes benefits that a business should consider when evaluating credit card programs for a given situation:

1. **Increase in the Number of Customers.** Many customers shop primarily with credit cards and will seldom make a purchase with cash. By recognizing that preference and advertising the acceptance of credit cards, a retailer or bank can offer customers a variety of payment options. Customers who cannot immediately access cash to buy items they need or want often facilitate their purchasing decisions (impulse buying) through the use of a credit card.

2. **Building of a Database and/or Mailing List.** The retailer or bank can increase the number of prospects to whom it sends promotional offers, announcements of new products, or additional product sales. Over time and across many industries, experience has proven that a retailer's most profitable and loyal customers are the ones who carry its credit card. You can read more about the powerful impact of database marketing in Chapter 16.

3. **Prompt Payment.** Retailers receive prompt payment for their credit sales (except for proprietary in-house programs), which greatly enhances their cash flow.

4. **Demographic Customer Information.** By using the known credit card customer base, banks and retailers are able to profile the consumers they are attracting. This will help their advertising and marketing efforts.

5. **Competitiveness.** In today's economic environment, banks and retailers alike must seek out every competitive edge. The decision to have a credit card program and which credit cards to accept at your retail location may place your business at a competitive advantage or disadvantage with others in your industry. This should not be taken lightly.

The term *incremental sales* or *incremental business* invokes much discussion throughout the credit card industry. In my career, I have had many opportunities to discuss, evaluate, analyze, project, predict, and guesstimate how much of the business done on a credit card program is "pure plus business." This is what is commonly referred to as incremental sales or incremental profit.

While there are many ways to develop statistical information that should give you a good feel for what is incremental, to my knowledge, there is absolutely no way to calculate this figure exactly. Many a CEO has asked me point-blank for a hard figure or a percentage; my invariable reply is that marketers who offer to provide these figures do not know what they are talking about. I can, however, provide my best estimate or gut feeling or several methods for evaluating the figures on hand that can lead to a relatively sound conclusion.

Often, I will explain that a credit card program is very much like advertising. The beautiful 48-page sales flyer that a store places in the Sunday newspaper obviously does not draw in every single customer who pays a visit during the following week. Some of those customers would have come in and made a purchase without receiving the sale flyer . . . so what percentage of the total sales is really incremental from that advertising effort? The only thing the retailer knows for sure is that if the flyers do not appear in the paper, sales will be inadequate. Credit cards are very much like that.

If you would like more information on incremental sales, or credit in general, the Purdue University Credit Research Center and the New York University Institute of Retail Management both have excellent departmental resources. Their experts have developed enormous amounts of historical data about the origins and development of retail credit. I have been privileged and honored to have attended and participated in several of their conferences and presentations over the years, always finding them informative and quite detailed.

FUTURE TRENDS

So where are credit cards going? Nearly 12 years ago, in a lively brainstorming session with my staff, we looked ahead and saw that credit card marketing, indeed all credit card activities, would no longer simply involve the acquisition of new card holders. A parallel, if you will, to advertising. In those days, if you wanted more sales, you simply printed more sale flyers . . . . But not any more. Costs have gone up, and losses and bad debts have multiplied; meanwhile, the competition is now everywhere fighting for what has become an almost flat consumer disposable income. That's why retailers and banks—in alarming numbers—are being bought, are downsizing, or are going out of business.

Ten years ago, we fully anticipated what has now happened: *The sharpest, most innovative companies have sharpened their marketing tools and have gone to battle.* In our brainstorming session, we referred to that phenomenon as the "coming credit card wars." It is no longer just a matter of whether a consumer will accept your credit card or not (and that has become an ever tougher challenge), but whether sufficient incentive exists for the consumer to use your credit card instead of a competitor's.

Just think of the wide range of marketing tools in use today that did not even exist a few years ago. Who would have thought a credit card issuer would pay you to use its card as Discover does? Credit card issuers did not give you bonus airline frequent-flyer mileage as Citibank now does. Neither did card issuers offer extra warranties like those currently offered by American Express to cover the loss of your merchandise. Frequent-buyer incentives are coming out of the woodwork, spawned by the airline industry, and are being copied by many banks and retailers alike. Credit cards with emotional appeal are another approach: Use your bank card and help your alma mater . . . or your church . . . or your favorite football team . . . really. Use your credit card for a major purchase at any number of retailers and pay no finance charge for a specified period of time or be entered into a sweepstakes.

And, just when you think everything has been thought of, you can now use your credit card and get a discount on long distance calls—not a telephone calling card—an AT&T bankcard. Shell Oil Company has introduced their Chemical Bank MasterCard, which earns you free gas when you use it.

Oh . . . and now General Motors has entered the credit card business giving customers a 5% rebate on a new GM car. General Electric has joined the field with the "Rewards MasterCard." Ford Motors joined forces with Citibank to counteract the GM card, and dozens of the nation's largest retailers have set up or are looking at setting up their own credit card banks. Well! Do those of you in the retail, bank, or T&E credit card business need this book? I think so.

The following chapters provide a category-by-category guide for the various credit marketing programs most successfully used by many banks, retailers, and other credit card companies today. In addition, I will give you scheduling guidelines to help you understand the required lead times involved in various programs. At the end of each chapter, I've included an "Ideal Program" that outlines the key points covered in that chapter.

The final chapter will explain how to develop and execute a successful credit marketing plan. Without a plan, your credit card program will not operate effectively and efficiently, and you will not generate the best return on your investment. Appendix A provides a sample marketing plan, and Appendix B lists vendor sources for different types of credit marketing programs.

In this revised edition of *Credit Card Marketing* (the first edition was published in November 1992), I have expanded and updated information in many chapters and have added new material that has become relevant in the mid-1990s. In today's economic environment, *those who understand how to get the most from their marketing investment* will be the ones around in a few years to talk about their success.

Let's start with my personal definition of successful marketing: "Providing the right product . . . at the right price . . . to the right person . . . at the right time . . . at the right place."

PRESCREENS AND PREAPPROVED SOLICITATIONS

Prescreening or preapproved programs can gain instant market penetration for your credit card program. Most banks, retailers, oil companies, finance companies, and other credit card issuers use prescreen or preapproved mailings as a primary method of account acquisition.

You have probably gone to your mailbox and found a letter from a bank, retailer, or other credit card company that says, "You have already been preapproved to receive our credit card with a credit limit of $xxx. Simply sign the enclosed form, mail it back in the enclosed envelope, and you will receive your credit card in the mail within a few days."

Most of these preapproved mailings include incentives for the customer to accept and then use the credit card.

Besides the preapproved offer by mail, you may receive a telemarketing call that advises you of your preapproved status and solicits your acceptance of a credit card.

Back in the late 1960s, prescreening did not exist. Several astute business people including A. J. Wood, Sr. and Irv Penner testified and lobbied before Congress to help make this marketing tool available.

The concept of a preapproved or prescreened program is relatively easy to understand but very complex to perform. It requires a coordination between vendor/partners, the credit bureau, your credit center, and many other departments. Meticulous attention to detail is essential, and the greater your understanding of demographic options, best approach, best offer, and so on, the more cost-effective you will be. Response rates have been declining for most industries over the past few years. This makes it more important than ever to use all the tools and experience available to maximize your return on investment.

When you perform a prescreen program, you select predetermined credit criteria such as these:

1. Number of credit references on file at the credit bureau.
2. Length of time these credit references have been on file at the credit bureau.
3. Delinquent history:
   - Never past due. Always prompt.
   - Two times 30 days late.
   - One time 60 days late.
   - Bankruptcy on file in the past 7 years.
   - Charge off.
4. Number of inquiries into the credit file within the past six months.
5. Type of credit references on file:
   - Revolving credit.
   - Finance company credit.
   - Mortgage company credit.

6. Beacon scores or other types of bankruptcy indicator scores.

Note: Any of the three major credit bureaus, CBI, TRW, or Trans Union will help you.

You have two more options. Select a credit bureau, give them your "prescreen criteria" (see preceding list), and request either of the following services:

1. Based on a physical location, such as a zip code, have the credit bureau extract names and addresses of consumers within that area who meet your predetermined credit criteria.
2. Furnish to the credit bureau consumer names for them to pass against their credit files to see which ones meet your predetermined credit criteria.

After completing the prescreen program, you still have to direct mail and/or telemarket the consumers who "passed" if you want to end up with new credit card accounts. Since any of the consumers who respond have already met your "ideal" credit requirements, you will not need to run another credit check. You will need to check the respondents' information, however, to be sure it is complete so that you can emboss and mail them their credit card. This last step is commonly referred to as the *back end*.

Approximately 10 years ago, Congress passed a law prohibiting the mailing of nonrequested credit cards to any consumer. Therefore, you must mail and/or call those consumers who passed your criteria to get their permission before sending them your credit card. Another key legal factor is the federal requirement that all consumers must receive full disclosure of the finance charges, repayment terms, annual fees, and other costs associated with your credit card prior to their use of that card. That makes it necessary for you to print these terms and conditions on the back of your pre-screen letter and/or include them with the credit card itself.

Now if all this sounds too complicated, keep in mind that:

> All credit promotions are profitable . . . if you can
> wait long enough.
>
> ~*Bill Grady*

This is a reminder that your prescreen program's rate of effectiveness can directly affect your company's bottom line.

For example, you might spend $100,000 for a prescreen or preapproved program. At a response rate of 10% to your direct mail offer, you would become profitable twice as fast as with a response rate of 5% (assuming equal activation rates).

Likewise, if 25% of those consumers who accepted your credit card activated it (used the card), becoming profitable would take twice as long as if 50% were to do so.

PRESCREEN SCHEDULING

Exhibit 2-1 is a step-by-step outline showing the major requirements for planning a preapproved or prescreen program.

To give you additional help executing the prescreen program, Exhibit 2-2 provides a chronological checklist of budget, direct mail, and telemarketing routines. By answering these questions, you will be able to determine most of the key information needed to perform a prescreen program. In going through the checklist, keep in mind that *there is no such thing as too much follow-up*.

Exhibit 2-1
Schedule for developing a prescreen credit card program.

Task	Time Frame
1. Initial selection of consumer names to be solicited	One to six weeks

  A. Sources:
- Customer list.
- Credit bureau extract.
- Compiled (rented) list of prospects.

  B. Possible requirements for list preparation:
- Securing source documents.
- Keying source documents.
- Formatting for credit bureau (tape specifications).
- Securing trade area analysis (how many names are available within your market).
- Studying demographics.
- Determining quantity of names available by zip and demographics.
- Prioritizing of zip codes for primary trade area.
- Using merge/purge against existing credit card base.
- Checking NCOA of list (national change of address verification).

(continued)

Exhibit 2-1 *(continued)*

Task	Time Frame
2. Credit bureau screen	Three to six weeks
A. Select credit bureau(s) to be used.	
B. Determine credit prescreen criteria to be used.	
C. Request bankruptcy or risk modeling score.	
3. Creative aspects—layout, design, copy for mail, or telemarketing package	Three to four weeks Start up front
A. Obtain quotations from vendors.	
B. Select your direct mail and telemarketing vendor/partner.	
4. Printing or computer fill and lettershop	Two weeks
5. First-class mail delivery; bulk rate mail delivery	One week Two weeks
6. Response time (mail)	Four weeks
7. Tape-to-tape processing; for mail responses; this is the back end.	Starts first week and ends one week after mail cutoff
8. Telemarketing	One to three weeks
A. Deduping of mail response.	depending on
B. Calling process.	number of accounts
C. Back end, same as mail	and acceptance rate
9. Emboss and mail cards	One to two weeks

Exhibit 2-2
Prescreen mail and telemarketing routines.

1. Determine the number of accounts needed.
2. Determine the program(s) to be used:
   - Direct Mail.
   - Telemarketing.
3. Mail:
   - First-class postage rate.
   - Bulk-rate postage.
4. Telemarketing—determine cost (per account).
5. Develop budget available for prescreen program.
6. Determine estimated schedule.
7. Determine locations/areas to be prescreened.
8. Determine customer list to be used:
   - Direct extract from credit bureau.
   - Existing customer list.
   - Rented list.
9. Determine demographics to be used—order trade area analysis if needed.
10. Contact vendor/partner for mail and telemarketing to assist in:
    - Layout and design.
    - Letter copy.
    - Cost estimates.
    - Back-end processing routines.
11. Secure budget approval if necessary.
12. Identify credit bureau(s) to be used.
13. Determine the credit limits you will be assigning.
14. Determine the prescreen credit criteria you will use and send this to the credit bureau(s) along with:
    - Number of consumers to be mailed.
    - Bankruptcy score matrix desired.
    - Contact person if outside list is used.

(continued)

Exhibit 2-2 *(continued)*

- Source of consumer names (extract or mailing list).
- Vendor/partner to send the output tape to and format requirements for the tape.
- Target date for vendor/partner to receive credit bureau tape.

15. Provide details of the prescreen program to all concerned parties—sending a sample to each of the following:
    - Your branches or retail locations.
    - Your credit card center, customer service, and operations departments.
    - Your embossing department.
    - Your third-party provider if there is one.
    - Your company's upper management.

16. Merge/purge your proposed prescreen consumers against your existing credit card account base.

17. Establish the cutoff date for your mail responses.

18. Be sure your legal department has approved the required disclosures for Truth in Lending laws.

19. Assign any tracking codes that your computer system or vendor/partner can accommodate to better evaluate your prescreen results.

20. Provide each vendor/partner involved with tape formats.

21. Coordinate and monitor final details:
    - Check special inserts in the prescreen mailing.
    - Check Truth in Lending disclosures to be inserted with the credit card when mailed to the consumer.
    - Make sure your business reply envelope has the correct bar codes and detail.
    - Supply a block of account numbers to your vendor/partner if you intend to preassign them.
    - Make sure your telemarketing vendor/partner gets a tape of mail responses to dedupe.
    - Prepare activation incentive coupons for insertion when credit cards are embossed and mailed.

SELECTING YOUR TARGET MARKET

Remember my definition of marketing in Chapter 1:

> Providing the right product . . . at the right price . . .
> to the right person . . . at the right time . . . at the
> right place.

Let's say you have a good product and the cost (annual fee or interest rate) is competitive, then who is the right person to receive your preapproved offer and when do you send it?

Here's a general rule of thumb: *Build peaks on peaks, not peaks on valleys.* This does not mean that you cannot freely choose when to run your prescreen program; however, if you promote just in front of a peak selling season, more consumers will react and respond positively to your offer than in an off-season or slower time of the year.

One of the most important decisions you will make regarding your prescreen program is, *Who* are you going to solicit? You learned earlier that you can extract names directly from the credit bureau or you can provide the credit bureau with the names to be prescreened. In either case, demographic information becomes invaluable. Just as the shotgun approach is no longer cost-effective in advertising, neither does it work well for credit card prescreen solicitations.

There are dozens of demographics for you to select from. Some examples are:

- Single-family homeowner.
- Multifamily homeowner.
- Apartment owners or renters.
- Income range (e.g., $25M to $50M).
- Hobbies or sports preferences.

You then determine the proximity of the consumer to your location. Are you in a rural market or a metropolitan market? Where do you pull your market share from? If you are marketing a T&E credit card, what professional segment do you target?

Then there is the most powerful consumer list of all—it comprises the names of prospects who are already your customers but do not yet have your credit card. In working with over 200 top companies in the United States, Canada, and abroad, I have found, without exception, that known customers of a business will respond at least twice as well as any other list of consumers the company can possibly obtain.

The following list ranks the effectiveness of response rates from best to worst, based on the source of your consumer list:

1. Known recent customers of yours (have been in your bank or retail location within the past 6 months) who have used another type of credit as their payment mechanism.
2. Known recent customers of yours (have been in your location during the past 6 to 12 months).
3. Known customers of yours.
4. Highly specific, targeted rental names that match the demographic and geographic profile of your existing best credit card customers.
5. Targeted rented list that fits the overall profile of your company's best customers (census data).
6. Partially demographically selected direct extract customer names from the credit bureau (e.g., income levels, homeowner).
7. Partially demographically selected rented customer names (e.g., income levels, homeowner).
8. Anybody within one to two miles of your company's physical location.
9. Anybody.

GUIDELINES ON COSTS AND RESULTS

Here are some of the questions most frequently asked by management and some general comments to help guide you.

Question 1. How much does it cost to conduct a prescreen program?

The total cost will depend on your specific needs and the various vendors you choose to use (see Appendix B). Cost will vary greatly from retailer to bank to oil company to T&E or other card-issuing company. It has a lot to do with the customer you are going after, the economic return you get from an active card holder, and the size of the prescreen program you undertake.

For example, your price per mail package is substantially lower for a 2-million-piece mailing than for a 25-thousand-piece mailing. Some credit bureaus may have a minimum charge. And while nobody gets a volume discount at the U.S. Post Office, a larger mailing concentrated in a smaller geographic area will have a higher percentage that will carrier route qualify, which does result in a lower postage cost.

Question 2. What will my response rate be?

Response rates vary tremendously based on industry as well as on your skill in following the ideal prescreen model at the end of this chapter. For example, some of the low-velocity, big-ticket retailers could get less than a 1% response and be very profitable. On the other hand, some high-velocity, small-ticket retailers could get a 5% response and be very unhappy. A general rule of thumb is the higher the average ticket (sale), the lower the response. Or, at a bank, given the annual fee involved, you can target a breakeven or profit goal.

Question 3. How much sales and profit will I get?

It can be hard to predict but easy to calculate the results after the fact. With many years of experience, I can project response rates or profitability for almost any industry within 5%. As you perform your prescreens and analyze the results of each, you will gain enough experience to forecast future results fairly accurately. In the meantime, this is another area where your vendor/partners can help you since they may have some related experience in your industry.

Likewise, the method of evaluating the success of a prescreen varies greatly. Some companies will base success on the response rate, some on the activation rate of those who respond, some on the immediate sales achieved, and some on the lifetime sales and profits derived from the prescreen. CFOs and accountants tend to look at the cost per account acquired. Sales and marketing executives tend to look at the sales per account acquired. Presidents and CEOs tend to look at the ROI.

SUMMARY

Prescreen programs can be very profitable if done properly but should not be the only method of account acquisition used. They do represent the fastest method available for instant market penetration or account acquisition. On the downside, they can also be expensive if the response rates or activation rates are low and prescreening requires an upfront capital outlay that will be recovered over time as sales and revenues are generated.

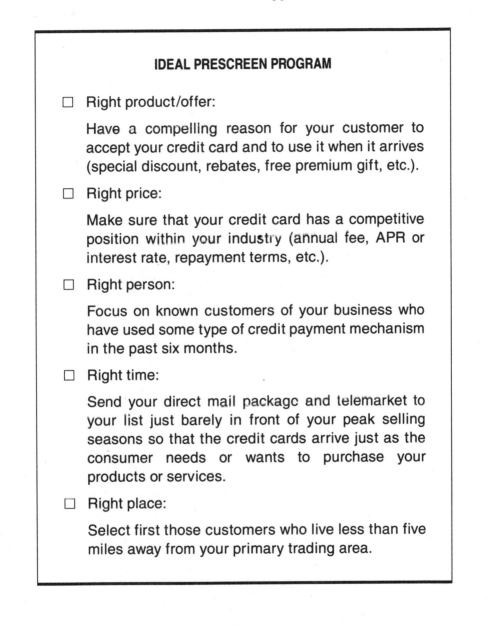

IDEAL PRESCREEN PROGRAM

☐ Right product/offer:

Have a compelling reason for your customer to accept your credit card and to use it when it arrives (special discount, rebates, free premium gift, etc.).

☐ Right price:

Make sure that your credit card has a competitive position within your industry (annual fee, APR or interest rate, repayment terms, etc.).

☐ Right person:

Focus on known customers of your business who have used some type of credit payment mechanism in the past six months.

☐ Right time:

Send your direct mail package and telemarket to your list just barely in front of your peak selling seasons so that the credit cards arrive just as the consumer needs or wants to purchase your products or services.

☐ Right place:

Select first those customers who live less than five miles away from your primary trading area.

"Take-One"
Applications

Some people may question why I would devote a chapter to a simple thing like "take-one" applications that are displayed in a plastic holder and are mailed in independently by the consumers who take them home. It is because over the years I have discovered the importance of how you market this program and its impact on credit card acquisition sales and costs.

Not every consumer will respond to a preapproved mailing. Not every consumer will fill out an application while in your bank or your store, even with the incentive of a free gift. Some people want to take an application with them, where in the privacy of their own home, on their own time schedule, they can complete the application and put it in the mail.

Of all the forms of account acquisition available to you, this one is the most cost-effective and you should always thoroughly promote it. After all, with this approach you don't pay up-front to do a preapproved mailing, and you don't give the customer 10% off or a free gift to apply for your credit card. All you really do is pay the business reply postage to receive the application in the mail.

Some companies (a very few) don't even pay the postage on take-ones, thinking that customers who want an account badly enough will pay the postage. I totally disagree. If you were distributing a five-dollar catalog you had available, then you might want to qualify the desire of the customer prior to just giving it away. When it is an inexpensive credit card solicitation that may represent more value to you as a business than it does to the customer, it is hard to justify skimping on postage. This is the same customer to whom you are willing to give a nice free gift or a big discount in return for a credit card application, incentives that certainly cost more than postage.

American Express figured out the value of take-ones years ago to the point that they pay retailers and others to promote them. They even have independent contractors whose job is to visit the locations of all the businesses that accept the American Express card, place application holders in prominent positions, and periodically refill them.

DESIGNING THE APPLICATION

The design of your take-one application is very important. Be careful not to clutter the front marketing panel so that customers cannot easily tell what they are looking at. Typically, the form includes a picture of the credit card, a few bullet points about the benefits of acquiring it, and a few action words such as *apply today, open an* (your store) *account,* or *become a preferred customer.*

The inside of the application is critical as well, not from the marketing and advertising aspect, but in the way the request for information is formatted. Design the application so that it is easy to follow. Leave enough room for applicants to actually write in the necessary information. Have you ever completed a form where the space provided for your name or address was so small that you had to write on the border, or on other parts of the form? It can be helpful to shade important parts (data you need for a short-form or instant credit procedure). In every case, ask only for information you need to make a credit decision or for future collection follow-up. For example, why ask for a relative's name and address if your collection department never uses the information or if your system does not capture it. The bottom line is to keep it simple and easy.

MARKETING CREDIT CARD APPLICATIONS

Now about the marketing of "take-one" applications. In my visits to hundreds of retail and bank locations, where I evaluate all forms of marketing, I am constantly amazed at the lack of attention paid to this key marketing tool. Some banks have absolutely no take-one applications on display. Some retailers have a few old, damaged, application holders at their checkout cash registers, but no credit card applications in them. Even worse, sometimes the holders are filled with other materials such as warranty information brochures, manufacturer product brochures, or sign-up forms for mailing lists. No wonder these companies get very few mailed-in applications.

Still other companies do a great job of displaying credit card applications at every cash register, at customer service departments, in their credit department, and at other strategic locations throughout their operation.

In choosing the credit card application holder, don't order just any holders. There are a few standard sizes for credit applications. If your application conforms to one of these sizes, your holders will be much lower in cost. Stay away from a custom-built holder, unless absolutely necessary, as it will be 10 to 20 times more expensive than a standard model. You will shorten the life of the holder if you build a theme or slogan into it. Themes and slogans tend to change over time. Look carefully at the space you can use at your cash registers and other locations before you select your holders. If only a small space is available, a large credit application holder may disrupt your checkout area.

There are lots of other opportunities for you to build your credit card base with take-one applications. Some of these are less effective than others so let's take a moment to look at a few different options and their viability.

Bag Stuffers.   Some companies will place their take-one applications in the bag with the customer's merchandise so that customer will take it home. Usually, so few customers complete and return these applications that the method will probably not be cost-effective except in an upscale, low-volume retail or service operation. In such businesses, the clientele often expect a higher level of service, usually use their credit card accounts for convenience, and would be more comfortable taking the application home without any interaction with the salesperson. In general, I would not recommend this method of distributing take-one applications; however, in some instances you might consider it.

Inserts into Flyers, Tabs, or Other General Direct Mail Packages.   This approach, while it sounds good in terms of numbers of credit card applications distributed, is usually very inefficient for several reasons. A very low percentage of consumers (2% or less) will complete a full credit card application received in mass mailings, advertising flyers, tabloids, or their newspaper. And, of those consumers who do complete the application, a high percentage are not creditworthy; they simply complete the application because of its easy availability through mass distribution. I do not recommend this use of take-one credit card applications.

Merchandising Shows, Fairs, and How-To Classes.   While nothing can match the success of an efficient in-store take-one program, specialty events can be the next most effective distribution. Some good examples are bridal fairs, food fairs, and consumer shows, such as home improvement or travel shows. Other opportunities exist with product demonstration or how-to programs sponsored by your company or by a particular industry. These events can be effective because they are somewhat more targeted to a particular audience. For example, if you are in the home center business, a home improvement show will attract your targeted customer. Nevertheless, the number of credit card applications completed and returned will be lower than the return rate for take-ones at your own business.

SUMMARY

Your take-one credit card application program can take on an air of marketing and promotion. For example, you can place toppers in the back of the application holder promoting a seasonal or credit theme, even promoting the take-one application itself: "Apply for our credit card account and be entered into our sweepstakes contest." With the decline in interest rates over the past few years, a number of banks have promoted a low APR as a reason to open a bankcard account with them.

Application holders can be designed and placed so that they complement the layout or decor of the store of bank. The holder can be placed on support posts, counters, items of merchandise, sales desks, information centers, consumer training schools, and booths used in home shows or other events. A good rule of thumb would be to place your application holders at any points of contact with customers, especially at all cash registers, customer service centers, and any high-ticket departments.

IDEAL "TAKE-ONE" PROGRAM

☐ Place credit card application holders at all checkout or transaction points throughout the store or bank.

☐ Place application holders in other strategic locations such as the second mortgage loan office, alongside big ticket products, and so on.

☐ Make sure you have enough applications in the holders.

☐ Always use business reply cards with postage prepaid.

☐ Design your application so it is uncluttered, easy to read, complete, and nonintimidating to consumers.

☐ Add toppers to the application holders. Change these two to four times per year with special themes or offers promoting the take-one application such as *No Annual Fee, No Payment for 60 Days,* or *Sweepstakes* entry.

☐ Use standard-size plastic application holders—not big poster board easels with holders built in. Remember, such displays are easily toppled space-eaters, a commodity that is at a premium near the cash register or checkout area.

INSTANT CREDIT

Instant-credit programs can be one of your best overall methods of maximizing your credit card marketing efforts. We need to start out by understanding what instant credit is.

Instant credit does not necessarily mean instant as the marketing nomenclature implies. For stores, it means being able to open a credit card account for customers while they are in the store so that they may take their purchase home with them that same day. That is precisely why instant credit is such a valuable tool.

Look at what you get from opening an account for a customer who is in your store. It is quick, maybe not instant, but surely much quicker than mailing in an application and waiting for a few weeks to be able to use it. It gives the retailer an immediate sales transaction, thus creating quick cash flow and gross margin dollars. It means 100% activation since these customers are applying to open and use the account right now so they can take products or services home with them. Plus, the first purchase amount of instantly opened accounts tends to be larger than the average sale amount.

These are all powerful benefits of instant-credit programs. On the downside, you have to deal with customers who are turned down for an account. This is not normally a big problem if you have done a good job of training your sales associates and have followed some key techniques that can help reduce the problem of declined accounts.

SETTING UP AN INSTANT-CREDIT PROGRAM

Let's look at how your instant-credit program is set up. From a marketing perspective, instant-credit programs can be set up in several ways:

1. **On-Line POS Instant Credit.** While at Service Merchandise, I initiated, through the POS (point of sale) cash register system, the first on-line instant-credit program used by a national retailer. Of all the options available, this one is the quickest and easiest to administer, and I am proud to have participated in its development. However, you must be in an on-line environment, have alpha-numeric capabilities at your POS cash register, and have access to sophisticated credit scoring algorithms for this to work for you.

2. **Off-Line Instant Credit.** In this case, you have the customer complete the credit card application and then send an abbreviated form of the application by fax or through a PC terminal to your credit center for evaluation and approval.

3. **Regular Processing.** Believe it or not, some companies actually check each instant-credit application as if it were a mail-in. Their credit center pulls a credit file and

scores the account, and a credit manager reviews the account for approval. After reaching a decision, the credit center calls the store with the disposition. This process may take two or three hours depending on the backlog in the credit card center.

4. **Calculated Risk?** Years ago, a number of companies used this approach and a few still do today. In this method, the customer is asked to provide positive ID, such as a driver's license, proof of employment, and a major credit card from a bank or T&E company. Other requirements may exist for various retailers. With this information in hand, the local store simply assumes the customer has good credit and opens the account on the spot without checking any credit files or performing any other credit evaluation functions. This may save the cost of credit bureau reports, but it also increases the possibility of fraud and higher bad debts.

No matter what method you use internally, consumers have come to understand that instant credit means you have a credit program available and that they may be able to open an account while at your place of business.

IMPLEMENTING THE PROGRAM

The following sections provide some tips to help you with your own instant-credit program.

Require Another Major Credit Card

Always require that the customer present another major credit card when applying for your instant-credit program. Preferably this will be a card that you accept for purchases.

If they are then turned down for an account, you may be able to put that particular purchase on the other credit card. It also means that they probably have a credit file.

Always Get a Positive Picture ID

Fraud runs rampant in today's society. Visa now allows you to put your picture on their credit cards, and holograms have been around for some time, all aimed at the enormous fraud problem.

Make the Application Short

In many cases, instant-credit customers did not come into your store to open an account. They found out about your credit card and its benefits from a sales associate or signs, or they just ran out of cash and asked. Long application forms have a very dampening effect on customers. Invariably, long and cumbersome applications will not be completely filled out anyway, but the requests for additional data will create some friction between your sales associates and their customers.

Many companies use shaded applications. Customers who mail in the application fill it out completely. For an in-store instant-credit application, only the shaded area needs to be completed. The abbreviated version saves additional time because the sales associates have to call in or enter this information into the computer system for processing. The shorter the application, the better for everyone.

Train Employees Thoroughly

Thoroughly train all employees in the use of your instant-credit program. This is one area that you should spend a lot of time with. If your program is performing less than satisfactorily, it is usually because your employees are unsure of or unfamiliar with its operation. Sometimes, they are not trained in how to handle declined applications and will not even offer instant credit because they fear the customer will not be approved.

Managers at one company I worked with explained that they had taken a group of their best credit people out to their stores and held extensive training the previous year. Instant-credit applications increased dramatically for a time but then had dropped off and were no better now. I asked what their employee turnover rate was. One of the managers replied that it was 55%, so we quickly realized that most of the people who had been trained were no longer with the company. We then put a video and training package together that was made a part of their company's new employee orientation program.

Advertise Your Instant-Credit Program

All flyers, tabs, ROP (run of press) newspaper ads, radio, TV, in-store signs, and so on, should make the consumer aware of this valuable option. By now, most consumers identify with the words instant credit, but they will seldom ask for the service unless you constantly advertise its availability. Sometimes our advertising manager will ask if we really need to show the credit card and instant-credit promotions on flyers, since he is more interested in putting only merchandise in front of customers. I quickly remind him that our credit card program represents a major percentage of the total sales, and it is a small amount of exposure for such a big part of the business.

Market the Program in Your Store

A good way to get year-round success with instant credit is to arrange a permanent credit application table in each store. This should be a library-size table high enough that customers who are standing up can write on it comfortably. Get a professional skirt to put around the table with something printed on it such as "Apply for Instant XYZ Company Account Here." Put applications and signs on the table with clear instructions for filling out the application. To add appeal, have a poster showing a free premium incentive or one-time discount that is available with a new instant-credit account. Your signage can instruct customers to take their completed application to customer service to have it processed and to receive their free gift.

If conditions permit, you can staff the table from time to time with a sales associate who can greet customers as an in-store hostess and invite them to open an account while they are in the store.

Another way to boost instant credit is to put the requirements for instant credit on the front of your take-one applications. Be sure they are brief and in bullet points.

IDEAL INSTANT-CREDIT PROGRAM

☐ Make the program as instant as possible—less than 5 minutes is a good target. If it is on line at a register, it should take 5 to 10 seconds.

☐ Advertise everywhere so your customers will know instant credit is available.

☐ Make it easy and fast for your sales associates to use.

☐ Make sure instant credit is a major focus of your marketing efforts, such as employee contests, credit signing, acquisition efforts, and hostess programs.

☐ Have a permanent hostess table in each store.

☐ Include the program in all training procedures for new employees.

In-Store Signs

In-store signage is often overlooked when preparing your credit marketing plans. Many retailers and banks do an excellent job, while others totally forget or ignore this powerful marketing tool.

Signs can be broken down into four categories:

1. Banners.
2. End-caps and easel cards.
3. Price tags.
4. Seasonal themes.

We will look at each of these categories and how you can use them to promote your credit card program successfully. Signage should be easy to read and easy to understand. Don't make things complicated, technical, or so cluttered that no one can catch the message in the few seconds it takes to pass by your signing.

My basic philosophy for in-store signage is:

Customers should not be able to walk through the front entrance of your store or bank and walk out the exit without becoming aware that you have a credit card program.

At the same time, your program should not overwhelm the store by inundating it with masses of oversized, brightly colored credit card signs that literally destroy the decor of your business or dwarf the other important signage.

BANNERS

These large signs normally hang from the ceiling or across a wall. Depending on the square footage of a particular location, only one or two should be used. Banners usually identify categories of products or services by saying something like "Instant Credit Available on the XYZ Credit Card" or "Only 9.4% APR on a New XYZ Visa Card."

Banners should always be broad and informational in content, not cluttered and detailed. They need to be brief and to the point. Banners should be made of durable material since they generally stay up much longer than most other in-store signs. If you intend to use them outdoors, be sure the banners are rainproofed and are constructed with wind vents so that the first storm that passes through does not demolish them. Banks use banners extensively and effectively to promote credit card offers.

END CAPS AND EASEL CARDS

Both in size and visibility, end caps and easel cards compose the next tier of store signs. End cap signs generally identify a small group of products or specific services.

A few of these signs should be placed in strategic locations. You probably will need 5 to 10 signs depending on the square footage of your store.

End cap and easel signs can present a more specific message than banners; for example, "90 Days Interest Free Available on our XYZ Credit Card . . . Free Trip to Disney World Sweepstakes entry each time you use your XYZ MasterCard . . . Apply here for an instant credit account." When using end cap and easel signs, you need to be ever mindful of the design, layout, and decor of your store. If you carelessly create bright red easel signs when the decor of your store is mauve and blue, the clashing colors may draw attention to your credit sign but they will also denigrate your company's efforts to design layouts with broad customer appeal.

PRICE TAGS

One of the best ways to give your credit card program regular and powerful exposure is to include it on your store's price tags. You can do this in a couple of ways. The first way is to preprogram or preprint onto the price tags a space for a monthly payment amount on the XYZ credit card. The second way is to print a message across the bottom of the price tag (e.g., Apply today for an XYZ account; Instant credit available; Use your XYZ credit card).

Price tags probably provide the marketing opportunity that retailers most often overlook. It is also the method that can cost the least while simultaneously getting the most exposure for your credit card program. It costs less because virtually all merchandise items carry a price sign or price tag. When you incorporate your credit card program into the sign, you are simply making more efficient use of what is already available.

All too often, we think our sales associates are mentioning the features and benefits of our credit card program to each and every customer. My experience over many years has been that this is just not true. Including a credit message on most of the item price signs ensures that customers know you have a credit card program.

SEASONAL THEMES

Most retailers and banks develop various promotions around specific events or holidays: Christmas, Independence Day, anniversary celebrations, and so on.

In-store signage packages created for these special events should include your credit card program as a tag line on several of the signs, or in a more prominent role. Some industries lend themselves to promotional signage packages that can be built around the credit card program itself. For example, you may run a 6-month, interest-free program that is the major focus of the overall promotion. Seasonal signage allows you to give your credit card program a fresh theme or different look regularly throughout the year. And, you work your credit card into a seasonal package, without incurring any additional cost.

There are a few other excellent credit card signage opportunities to keep in mind. Front door decals indicating the credit cards you accept are a must. Signs at your checkout points or cash registers should indicate the credit cards you accept as well as any special credit card procedures you may have for your customers. This item may seem to be insignificant, but it is crucial for the customer who needs to know and won't ask. On several of my tours, I have found retail operations where the only card with any visible signage was the

American Express card, even though the store had its own credit card and also accepted Discover, MasterCard, and Visa.

Another opportunity for advertising your credit card program within the store is through the use of cardboard signs called *toppers.* These signs are designed to slide into the back of take-one credit card application holders and are useful for drawing attention to take-one applications or special promotions, for example, "Use your XYZ card today and help your favorite charity," or "Instant Credit Available." Toppers are very inexpensive and can be changed frequently.

The most important "credit card" sign you have year-round is the front panel of your take-one application. No matter what type of credit card you have—Visa, MasterCard, or private label—that front panel is probably the "sign" seen by the most people in the most locations within your bank or store. Therefore, think of it as a very important advertising and marketing and signage tool.

Keep your message on the front of your application short and eye-catching, usually with a picture of your credit card as the center focus. Avoid cluttering the panel with paragraphs of copy. Use bullet points, and only important bullet points. Use attractive colors that will blend with your company's image. Avoid slogans that will outdate your applications if your company changes themes (which all companies do rather frequently).

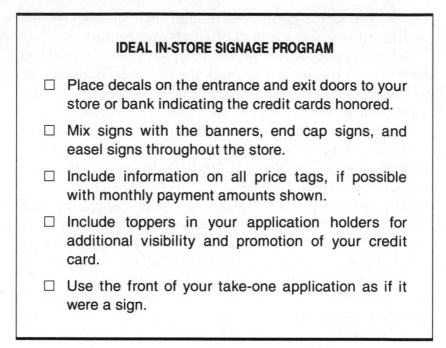

IDEAL IN-STORE SIGNAGE PROGRAM

☐ Place decals on the entrance and exit doors to your store or bank indicating the credit cards honored.

☐ Mix signs with the banners, end cap signs, and easel signs throughout the store.

☐ Include information on all price tags, if possible with monthly payment amounts shown.

☐ Include toppers in your application holders for additional visibility and promotion of your credit card.

☐ Use the front of your take-one application as if it were a sign.

HOSTESS PROGRAMS

Hostess programs, sometimes referred to as *direct solicitation* programs, can yield some of the best credit card accounts available. Hostess programs also lend themselves to certain one-of-a-kind opportunities that do not exist with other credit marketing efforts.

In its simplest definition, a hostess program means that a company employee or a professional hostess vendor/partner company solicits consumers, in person, to complete an application for your credit card. These programs usually offer a premium or other incentive to help make the solicitation as successful as possible.

Accounts acquired through hostess programs usually have better than average approval rates, activate quicker, and have higher overall activation rates than most other forms of credit card acquisition.

To properly cover this important marketing program, this chapter addresses the application of hostess programs for banks and retailers separately.

HOSTESS PROGRAMS FOR BANKS

In general, bank-issued Visa and MasterCard credit cards are universally accepted and are not as location restricted as proprietary or retail credit cards. With banks, the major objective in choosing a location for a hostess program is the creditworthiness of the applicant. Upscale malls have proven to yield large numbers of reasonably creditworthy prospects. However, the mall management can be very restrictive regarding permission to approach consumers. Hostess booths at home and garden shows can attract a pool of creditworthy applicants. Strong support signage is essential, and booth counters must be high enough for convenience and productivity in assisting customers to complete applications.

Canadian banks do not have the drive-through windows that are so prevalent in the United States. All their customer traffic flows through the bank lobby, and since many Canadian banks are attached to malls, they have a lot of traffic. For this reason, hostess programs have been very successful at the bank entrance to the mall.

While U.S. banks do have drive-through windows, which reduce lobby traffic, the larger bank branches still provide enough lobby traffic to support a hostess program.

Banks that only issue credit cards are more limited since they have no bank premises; however, malls, trade shows, and home shows are still good locations for them to have hostess programs.

Certain affinity cards can be solicited very effectively when targeted directly to the affinity group. For example, all the NHL, NFL, and NBA teams have Visa or MasterCard programs. A hostess program conducted at their games can successfully attract loyal fans with the appropriate logo on a related item. Certain trade shows provide opportunities to solicit new credit card accounts relating to segments of the industry involved.

Hostess bankcard programs, like retail programs, generally require a premium incentive to produce reasonable numbers of applications. If there is an annual fee, the premiums should be more upscale than those used in retail card solicitations. To be effective, these premiums should probably be from $2 to $4 in price. Even without an annual fee, premiums always increase the number of applications obtained. The key is to keep the credit card as the main focus, not the premium item.

RETAIL STORE HOSTESS PROGRAMS

Promoting your company's retail credit card at the store level is vitally important to increase market share or to maintain the share you have. There are two distinct types of retail store hostess programs: (1) the professional hostess program, which utilizes the expertise, training, and professionalism of a reputable vendor/partner; and (2) the in-store employee program (not to be confused with employee contest).

Consider a hostess program for the following events:

- Grand openings.
- Remodeling re-grand openings.
- Mall events.
- Holidays.

HOSTESS PROGRAM USING PROFESSIONALS

This professional hostess program is provided by a reliable, professional outside vendor/partner at your store location or other designated location. A premium or free gift should be included to ensure maximum results.

While using an outside company appears to be more expensive (cost per application received) than using your own store personnel, the results will usually more than justify the investment. It takes a very special person to perform what amounts to cold-call selling. Such salespeople must be highly motivated, not easily discouraged, and focused on high production. At the same time, they must maintain the highest level of professionalism in dealing with customers. They must achieve a real balance in being assertive, but not aggressive, while always remaining professional and motivated throughout several days of high-energy, intense selling.

The best, most responsible hostess vendor/partner companies hire this type of person. You should utilize one of these companies to perform hostess programs during peak traffic times such as grand openings. The hostess company's focus will be on producing the most credit card applications possible since their people, unlike your own store employees, do not have to contend with other distractions.

Probably your most important task when planning a hostess program is selecting the hostess company itself. Reputable hostess companies will only send experienced teams, who are comfortable in the highly volatile atmosphere of grand openings and other major events. They also will be professional in their approach and will be appropriately attired, important considerations if the top executives of your company are likely to visit your store during the grand opening.

Let me give you an example. A retail operation used instore employees to execute a hostess program during the grand opening of one of its new stores. A free premium was provided to customers who applied for their credit card. At the end of the four-day grand opening, employees had taken a total of 39 applications. For the next grand opening, the firm used an outside hostess firm. With similar traffic, the hostesses generated more than 4,500 applications.

HOSTESS PROGRAM USING STORE PERSONNEL

A second option is to use your own employees to serve as hostesses. This method can work, but only if you plan your program properly and monitor it closely. There are instances where this approach may be preferable to hiring a professional hostess company, but it will probably be somewhat less effective.

Here are some of the pitfalls that you may run into.

- Generally, most store employees are not experienced in cold-call selling.

- Generally, most store employees will burn out quickly.

- Store employees have other primary responsibilities and will probably allow the hostess effort to take a backseat.

- Store management may constantly suspend the hostess effort by pulling employees to run cash registers or perform other pressing duties.

- Since store employees are not paid primarily for this hostess effort, the applications may often be incomplete and therefore of no value (the hostess company must provide complete applications to receive payment).

Does this mean that you cannot or should not use store employees ever? No. It means you must evaluate the importance of the program you have in mind and then determine whether to hire a hostess company or use your own store employees. Remember, you normally will get less productivity from the store employees than from the outside hostesses.

The following suggestions will be helpful in developing an internal (store employee) hostess program:

1. Use a slightly better premium (free gift).
2. Rotate employees frequently.
3. Watch for the employees who do the best job and focus on using them.
4. Pay a bonus to your employees for completed applications.
5. Check the applications on a regular basis to be sure they are being completed properly.
6. Purchase library-height tables from a hostess company to make it easier for your customers and your employees to complete applications. Sitting down promotes resting and congestion and decreases production.
7. Provide constant recognition of the goals met and results to help keep your employees motivated.
8. Do not allow your store management to divert employees designated for the hostess booth to other duties.

IDEAL HOSTESS PROGRAM

☐ Use a professional, reliable hostess vendor/partner if your budget permits it.

☐ Always provide a free premium incentive for the customer.

☐ Locate the hostess table just inside the main store entrance, where most customer traffic walks past. Take caution not to completely block the entrance.

☐ Use a library-size table, which is high enough to permit the customer to stand comfortably while completing the credit card application. This also reduces congestion.

☐ Schedule the hostess program for the duration of the major event, covering the maximum traffic flow, such as the first four days of a grand opening.

☐ Conduct the hostess program in conjunction with other credit marketing programs such as a pre-screen.

PREMIUMS

Premiums are a fascinating credit marketing tool. My experience as vice president of sales promotion for one of the nation's largest retailers and my earlier training in direct marketing and catalog programs gave me experience with premiums.

Time after time, premiums were effective in activating, reactivating, and acquiring new credit card accounts, as well as in stimulating sales. My first encounter was some 17 years ago when I tested a promotion that used a gift (premium) to stimulate a purchase instead of the usual 20% off discount. My goal was not the abolishment of discounts because they have a place; however, customer response to the premium offer was as effective as the discount. This was enlightening because the average sale for that promotion was usually $100 which meant the 20% discount cost us $20 of margin. In contrast, the premium we used for that program cost us $5, representing a remarkable $15 savings. Since then, I have regularly explored a balance of offers that always includes a strong look at any premiums that may fit our marketing objectives.

Over the years, I have worked with many marketing programs that involved premiums. They are not fail-safe. To improve your chance of success, you need to pay attention to some important guidelines. Here are some of the reasons premiums often rival discounts or other forms of sales incentives:

- Premiums have a high perceived value.
- Some customers prefer a gift to discounts or other incentives.
- You can pass along a better value for the cost. Since the customer is getting the premium at a volume cost price, the real value is much greater.
- The total cost to your company is usually less than for an offer of equal value (e.g., a 15% discount on $100 or $15) is more costly than a $5 premium with a perceived value of $15.
- By romancing the premium product, you can create an appealing presentation for your advertising approach, which will make your direct mail or other advertising vehicle look better than a simple discount coupon.

There are other costs and considerations to be aware of when using a premium. You must inventory the premium, and there will be some shrinkage (inventory loss) as with your regular merchandise. Employees sometimes think that because it is a gift the item can be given free for other purposes. This means that you will have some additional handling costs, but the savings will usually far outweigh this expense.

Premiums can be used for a variety of credit marketing programs.

ACCOUNT SOLICITATION

Premiums really help an in-store hostess program. The premium—a low-cost but worthwhile perceived value—is used as a gift to customers who complete a credit application while in your bank or store. Any in-store hostess program always will enjoy greater success with a premium. However, be sure to limit its value or customers will complete your credit card application just to get the gift.

You can place a sign near the main entrance to your building informing customers that they can receive a gift for completing a credit card application while in your store or bank (a silent hostess program). A small premium will also give your employees a reason to mention your credit card program since they will have something *free* to offer customers for their trouble. You will also find that the sign by itself, if placed on a table with a poster showing the free gift available, will increase your in-store application volume significantly. Be sure to have applications, pens, and other information on the table at all times. A library-size waist-high table enables customers to complete the applications without having to stoop excessively.

ACTIVATION AND REACTIVATION PROGRAMS

The activation of new accounts is critical to recoup the investment of adding new cardholders to your credit card base.

Accounts that have been acquired by direct mail and telemarketing need early attention if they are not activated. A good method is to offer new cardholders a premium incentive for the first use of their new credit card. You can advertise the offer on the bottom panel of your card carrier where it will be easily seen and can be removed for redemption. Or, you can include an insert with the new credit card mailing if the card carrier has inadequate space for the offer.

I cannot stress enough the importance of getting a new account activated as soon as possible. You should consider not only premiums but discounts and other one-time free services to entice your new cardholders to use your credit account. Most effective is a series of offers, each stronger than the last until you finally succeed in activating the account or move it into the nonmarketed file for occasional direct-mail or advertising use.

For reactivation or an additional boost to your active card base, you can include an insert in your monthly billings encouraging customers to redeem a gift by making another purchase on their credit card account.

You can use several methods of communicating your premium offer. Many companies use direct mail packages and enclose coupons. Others have found that postcard mailings with a full color picture of the premium on the front and the redemption procedures on the back are cost-effective and work well.

SELF-LIQUIDATING PREMIUMS

Some banks, retailers, and oil companies use self-liquidating premiums. You may have seen an offer for a set of ice tea glasses for only $1.00 with a fill-up of gasoline. How about a cuddly teddy bear, a $24.99 value for only $7.00 with a purchase of $50.00 or more at your mall department store? These are usually pretty good sales and activation stimulators, not quite as good as the *free* gift, but they can be effective if you do your homework. The biggest advantage of a self-liquidating premium marketing program is that your customers basically cover the cost of the premium, which keeps your total sales promotion cost down significantly.

If you pursue a self-liquidating premium promotion, be careful not to load up heavily on inventory that you may not be able to use. Better still, try to negotiate the right to return unused premium items at the end of the promotion. Self-liquidating premiums can be good activation and sales promotional tools as long as you don't overdo them or buy so much inventory that you end up giving a large quantity away.

PREMIUM GUIDELINES

1. Select a premium that will appeal to men or women, or both, as appropriate.
2. Select a premium that is disposable and needs to be replaced or a premium that is always useful, even if you have more than one (e.g., a flashlight).
3. Stay away from gimmicks.
4. Stay away from cute, unusual trinkets.
5. Select a premium with the appropriate perceived value for your marketing objective. For example, if you are trying to motivate someone to buy a brand-new Lincoln Continental, a pen and pencil set is a little weak.
6. Select a premium that is not too high for the objective of your marketing plan. For example, don't use a $50 set of Corning Ware to get a credit card application completed. Customers with no interest in the card will fill out the application to get their gift.
7. Test new premium items against your best-performing item.
8. Consider giving consumers a choice of premiums.

Premiums can be a lot of fun if you will follow these guidelines. In every case, be careful to select a reputable, financially sound premium vendor/partner who has experience in the credit industry. In most cases, premium vendors have access to specially packaged or unique products. They may resemble products carried by your store; however, rarely would you be able to purchase the same item within your own buying group or at a lower price. Even though you may get a lot of pressure to use merchandise your business already carries, or discontinued merchandise, try to avoid this practice as the products to be used are rarely as effective as truly promotional items.

There was a company that selected a charcoal grill lighter as an account solicitation premium in spite of another more appropriate candidate (a flashlight). To show you how the preceding list can provide guidelines, let's review this item. Is it applicable to men and women . . . possibly. High perceived value? Do you know the value of a charcoal grill lighter? Do you have one already, or worse, do you even have a grill? Is it a gas grill? It can be used up, but I don't need two. As a result of this promotion, the company still has some charcoal grill lighters on hand after two years.

They followed this premium up with the same quantity of flashlights. Could you use another flashlight? Is the perceived value pretty good as an account solicitation premium? Would men or women want or need a flashlight? All the flashlights were gone within one month!

One last important thing to remember. When you find a premium that works well for you, use it until you find a premium that pulls better or until the effectiveness of the best producer begins to decline. Although this may seem obvious, you would be surprised at how many companies find a winner, use it once, and move on to try and find another winner without getting the most mileage possible out of the proven item. Keep testing new premiums constantly, but until you find one that beats your current offer, keep using your winner.

IDEAL PREMIUM PROGRAM

☐ Make sure the premium has a high perceived value for the actual cost paid.

☐ Use a premium that will be desired by both men and women.

☐ Offer something that your customers will want *even* if they already own an item like the one you're offering—such as a flashlight.

☐ Make your premium easy to inventory and control.

☐ Offer enough of a value to get your customer to respond.

☐ Offer a premium whose quality is in line with your products or services and will not pull down your image.

☐ Try to get the same response rate or activation rate as your other marketing efforts for less cost.

New Resident Programs

Nearly every segment of the corporate world uses new resident programs. People who are relocating, buying a new home, or moving to a new city (or just across town) represent an enormous marketing opportunity.

Much of the time, these consumers need more of everything after completing their move. Not only do they need products and merchandise, but they must identify new sources for many everyday services. Major purchases may include new carpet, paint, home improvement items. You may no longer know just where to find the friendly neighborhood grocery store, the dentist, a new doctor, or even a quality restaurant. Perhaps you will replace that old furniture, especially since it was damaged in the move. New bank . . . you bet! We could go on and on, but the point is that someone who moves is a unique marketing opportunity regardless of that person's demographic profile.

The new resident may already have been your customer before the move, but don't assume that everybody knows who you are and where you are. Several times over the years, I have heard the comment, "Everybody knows our company and where we are; after all we have been in business here for a hundred years." Nothing could be further from the truth than that belief, especially in today's mobile society. It is estimated that from 20% to 30% of the working population now relocates each year. Just think about the last time you moved. How long did it take you to discover that your favorite clothier, restaurant, retailer, or bank had a branch or franchise in your new city?

Nearly every bank or retailer has some sort of new resident or new mover program in place, usually within the corporate advertising department, which is just fine. Sometimes, however, the marketing effort fails to inform the relocated consumer about the availability of a credit card.

On the other hand, the new resident program may be targeted specifically for soliciting a credit card. That is OK, but a dual approach is best. You invite the consumer to come into your place of business, and you offer them your credit card.

You can use many sources to find these newcomers:

- Real estate transfers of title (deed names).
- Utility turn-ons.
- Changes of address from credit bureaus.
- Changes of address from magazines.
- Changes of address from the post office (NCOA-National Change of Address System).
- New telephone listings.

Some vendors compile or rent data from one or more of these sources. Different vendors offer different options or selection criteria. For example, you should determine whether timing is critical: Is it important to reach a new resident as fast as possible?

For some businesses, the earlier you can put your offer in front of new residents the better. For other businesses, it may be more important to preapprove credit first, which will delay the access to qualified new resident customers by two to four weeks. If timeliness is everything, are you going to mail or telemarket to them weekly?

Several organizations make use of this type of data, such as the Welcome Wagon and political or civic organizations.

TARGETING CONSIDERATIONS

Like other credit promotions, new resident solicitations can be targeted to maximize your results. Targeting issues include:

- How will you eliminate your existing cardholders from the program? This is more complicated for new movers since their new address probably is not on your house file yet. You may have to conduct the merge/purge process at the old and new address to eliminate existing customers.
- Do you want to solicit new residents moving into apartments? Some sources (e.g., deed names) will not identify apartment dwellers. If this group is attractive, you may have to utilize additional sources.
- Is income targeting important? Most newcomer lists can be segmented by income level so you can isolate those movers who are most attractive to your business.
- What other demographic selections are needed? Some of the files can be selected by gender or move distance, as well as other variables.
- How is geographic targeting done? Your best results will come from those new residents moving into your primary trading areas. Is this done by market, SCF, zip code, or carrier route?

PRESCREENING THE NEW RESIDENT

Some companies want to limit their solicitation to pre-screened or prescored groups. This is a bit more challenging for new residents than a normal prescreen program because of the relatively small number of names involved, the need to match credit data with both the former and new addresses, and the time involved to perform the prescreen function at the credit bureau.

All together, the preapproval process will make the cost of your new resident program much higher and simultaneously reduce the number of potential customers. You can overcome the reduction of available names by sending two different offers, one that is preapproved for your company's credit card and one that simply invites the new resident to visit your business. Whether to use the prescreened approach or not requires careful consideration by your management. What is best for some financial businesses could be the wrong approach for certain retailers.

MARKETING OPTIONS

You can take any number of marketing approaches—from mailing a credit card application along with an invitation to visit your business to offering a special discount if the customer will accept your credit card account and use it at your location. In addition, businesses may present some type of free product to new residents who stop by to get acquainted. Some companies simply send a nice "welcome to the neighborhood" letter or postcard. However, a free gift, discount, or other offer is usually more effective.

Assume for the moment that you have studied your demographic options and selected the best new residents to market to and their proximity to your location. Further, you have prepared what you feel to be a good compelling reason (offer) for potential customers to visit your business. There remains at least one marketing process that is often overlooked but is extremely important. Your direct mail package or your telemarketing script should clearly inform the potential new customer about your business.

Have you ever received a direct mail preapproved credit package from XYZ company that included lots of great financial options and compelling reasons for opening a credit card account but did not supply the foggiest clue to the kind of business it operates? You may think this scenario is an exaggeration, but it happens every day. Unless the name of the business identifies the products or services offered, such as "First National Bank," potential customers have little incentive to accept the offer of an account from an unknown company.

Many big regional retailers may find it hard to believe that everyone does not know what they sell, but let's just suppose that I have a company in California named "Grady's" with 20 stores that have sold hundreds of millions in clothing business since 1900. If you had just moved to California from the East Coast and received an attractive preapproved new resident credit card offer from "Grady's," what type of business would you assume it was? A furniture store? A grocery store? A home furnishings business? (See what I mean?) So an important element of a new resident offer should be a brochure describing your company's products and services. This will always give some lift to the response rate of your program.

COSTS

The actual cost of your new resident program will be up to you and the vendor/partner you select since expenses can vary greatly depending on the nature of your business or service and whether your offer includes a preapproved solicitation or a credit application for the prospect to complete and mail in.

The cost per solicitation will be higher than other direct mail programs, but it is also much more targeted and unique. In addition, most new resident programs tend to have higher response rates, higher approval rates, higher activation rates, and spend more dollars than the average account.

When you evaluate all the preceding factors, you will usually find that the new resident program is just as cost-effective per new active account, if not more so, as many of your other credit marketing promotions.

IDEAL NEW RESIDENT PROGRAM

☐ Make sure the program is constant from month to month and year to year.

☐ Concentrate on your primary trading area.

☐ Carry both an offer for your credit card account (either preapproved or not) plus an offer to come to your place of business.

☐ Use only a proven, dependable vendor/partner who has experience in the credit card industry.

☐ Include a brochure to describe the products or services your company provides.

PART II

ACTIVATION PROGRAMS: GETTING CUSTOMERS TO USE CREDIT CARDS

ACTIVATION AND RETENTION
PROGRAMS

There are any number of ways to activate and keep active your credit card account base. You should always plan activation programs simultaneously with your acquisition programs. One sure way to create an expense burden and a drag on your ROI is to concentrate solely on account acquisition and rarely communicate with cardholders after they receive their card. Some companies have enormous credit card bases, but alarmingly low activation rates. You have made an enormous investment in building the card base, and you want to take advantage of that investment by marketing to these customers.

A well-run credit card program will be like the pistons of an automobile constantly alternating acquisition and activation, never concentrating on only one or the other. In this chapter, we will explore a number of activation programs. Some of the areas of discussion will cross lines with direct-mail and database programs.

The best time to think about activation programs is when you are planning the acquisition of credit card accounts. Study after study in many industries shows that the longer the period that elapses between acquisition and activation of an account, the harder and more expensive it is to get the customer to use account. For example, it is much more cost-effective if your newly acquired accounts react to an activation offer that they receive with their new credit card than if you spend months sending offer after offer. At the same time, as the months go by and the new account fails to activate, it becomes increasingly less likely that they will ever activate.

Your maximum window of opportunity is generally two selling seasons—a minimum of 12 months to a maximum of about 18 months. The exceptions to this rule are the large-ticket durable goods industries (e.g., furniture or lawn tractors).

HOW TO ACTIVATE CREDIT ACCOUNTS

To plan the best possible approach to activation follow these steps:

1. **Starting with the acquisition of the account, you might make an offer when the account is opened in the store.** This serves both an acquisition and activation purpose, and several department stores and others do this today. Usually this is an offer of 10% or 20% off that day's purchases on the customer's new credit card account. Banks can effectively do this by requiring or requesting an automatic cash advance check triggered by the acceptance of their bankcard.

   If you offer customers the option of opening instant-credit accounts while they are in your store, simply require that a purchase be pending to qualify and process such applications. Otherwise, you may mail their application in for future processing.

2. **Include an activation offer with the new credit card.** Regardless of the activation offer, many customers do not open their account in the store. The most economical to reach all cardholders (even if the accounts opened within the store get two offers) is to have an offer to activate on the bottom panel of the credit card carrier. This puts your activation offer right beside their new credit card. Usually, discounts, interest-free periods, or premium gifts are used; however, at times special privileges such as free gift wrap or delivery can work equally well.

   For many reasons, this will be the most cost-effective activation program you will ever use. You have to send the credit card anyway, and you must use a credit card carrier to hold the card in place and avoid damage. The printing of your activation offer on the bottom panel of the credit card carrier will not add any additional postage, printing, or paper costs to the package. And finally, this is one of the few times you will mail something to your customer by first-class postage, which helps ensure faster and better delivery than the third-class bulk rate normally used for mail activation or sales promotional offers.

3. **Offer a special private sale or closed-door event.** This is a good way to attract those people who have not activated within the first three months and to stimulate additional sales with those who are active. These events offer hot prices and special values for your preferred credit card customers. Here are some examples of these activation programs and how they would work:

- A two-hour exclusive sale only open to your preferred credit card customers. If your store typically closes at 7 P.M. or closes early Sunday, or opens at 10 A.M., you would schedule to open during two hours that are not normally available to the public. Put together a strong mailer that features compelling merchandise offers, extra discounts, free coffee and doughnuts or other snacks, a door prize drawing, and so on. Make these strong special offers only during this two-hour period and only to your credit card base. It is the sense of urgency and the privilege of having your store personnel and facilities available just for your special credit card customers that will have the most appeal, assuming good compelling offers.

- Another version of the special sale event is to have the specials available over a two- to four-day period, but only to cardholders when they present your special mailer within your store. The advantages are that customers can come in at their convenience and retailers have no additional hours of staffing; however, the sense of urgency is much less. To entice credit card customers to respond, you want to have the same compelling offers in either case.

4. **Send another mailing with a stronger offer.** By the end of the first six months, if the new account is still inactive, you may want to send a direct mail package to the account with a much stronger offer than those previously used. For example, you may regularly offer 10% off the first purchase when new customers receive their credit card. Now you may want to offer the accounts that did not activate a discount of 20%. If you offered a discount on your card carrier to which the new customer did not respond and likewise they do not respond to a larger discount, then it is time to

try offering a premium gift with their first purchase on the new account. If a premium does not work, then try offering a free service such as gift wrap or free parking.

I worked with a company that had religiously sent a 15% discount card to inactive accounts every quarter for over two years. The first time they mailed the postcard, they had obtained pretty good results. But after that, responses and sales had declined steadily. In our meetings, we discussed the fact that an inactive cardholder who has received several 15% off offers is unlikely to be motivated by yet another 15% discount. We then planned a free premium offer, mailed the same postcard format to those same inactive accounts. The response and sales went through the roof. And, the cost of the premium was substantially lower than the 15% discount, had it been utilized.

5. **Offer a mystery sale or discount.** Send your inactive account a game card or rub-off on a postcard or letter offering them the chance to get a prize or discount, possibly a grand prize or discount, which is hidden on your marketing piece. The advantage to this activation offer is the perception that you may win a major prize or large discount. If you plan this type of activation properly, it can give you an enormous return in sales and activation. To be sure it works at its highest level, do not have any losers. On your marketing piece, state, "You can win from 5% to 100% off your next purchase with this card." In your instructions, tell your customers to come to your store, select their merchandise and, at the cash register, give the rub-off card to the cashier to remove the secret seal that covers their discount. Even though most customers realize they are unlikely to get 100% off, they

know that they will at least get a 5% discount and maybe more. This perception, combined with actual savings, makes the offer very appealing.

ACTIVATE NEW ACCOUNTS DURING PEAK SELLING TIMES

The important thing to remember about activation is that it is urgent to activate new accounts as soon as possible and that to do so you should try a variety of different types of promotions and offers. Other concepts can improve your success as well. Be ever aware of timing—seasonal impact, holidays, and anniversaries—as these can only serve to help any activation program you choose. For example, a strongly priced three-day preferred sale on air conditioners will do incrementally better in the hot months of July or August than it will do in December or January. In other words, build peaks on peaks, not peaks on valleys, whenever possible. It is much more effective to get customers to activate when a particular buying season is underway than to do so during the off-season.

MAXIMIZING YOUR RESULTS

To maximize your ROI from the investment in your credit card base, your comprehensive activation and retention plan should treat your entire credit card base as inactive. In other words, make sure you are talking to your entire card base in some fashion during the course of a year.

Studies have proven that active accounts react better to your promotional efforts. You might send them an invitation to come in and shop. Recently inactive accounts should get a stronger promotional offer. Last, the hard-core inactive accounts receive your strongest offer.

In addition to your own credit marketing efforts, your company's other advertising efforts should always include your credit card base. If you mail sale flyers, then your credit card holders should receive the flyers. Monthly credit card billing inserts should always be used to stimulate add-on sales. If your company produces seasonal or annual catalogs, always send them to your credit card customers.

Don't fall into the trap of using only one type of offer. Consider the concept of wave mailings: This is a series of mailings using a variety of offers until you find the right combination to activate the maximum number of your credit card accounts. Don't just ignore them after they activate; follow up and keep them active.

There is a point in time after perhaps 12 to 24 months, when you discontinue mailings to your inactive accounts because you just cannot get enough response from them to be profitable. After spending a fairly substantial amount of time and money and offering the best incentives you have, set these accounts aside and do not include them in future credit activation programs. You want to maintain the customer information for other uses such as sending sale flyers or catalogs because these customers may respond to your general sales promotions.

By this time, you have established that these consumers have no interest in using their credit card account with you, and further expenditures on your part simply waste your available resources, which could be better spent on your active credit card customers. In Chapter 16, we will go over several ways to dissect your card base and utilize the various levels of active or inactive credit card customers most effectively for your business.

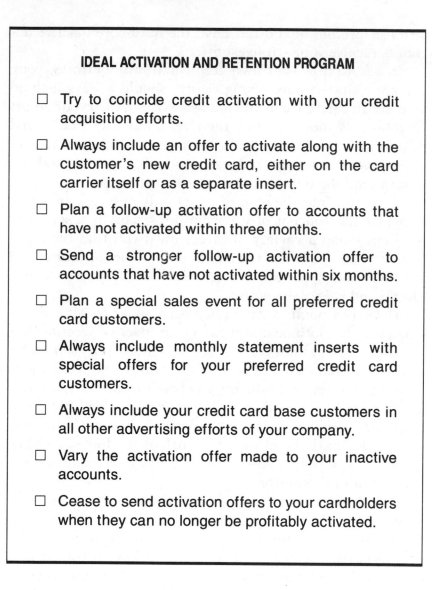

IDEAL ACTIVATION AND RETENTION PROGRAM

☐ Try to coincide credit activation with your credit acquisition efforts.

☐ Always include an offer to activate along with the customer's new credit card, either on the card carrier itself or as a separate insert.

☐ Plan a follow-up activation offer to accounts that have not activated within three months.

☐ Send a stronger follow-up activation offer to accounts that have not activated within six months.

☐ Plan a special sales event for all preferred credit card customers.

☐ Always include monthly statement inserts with special offers for your preferred credit card customers.

☐ Always include your credit card base customers in all other advertising efforts of your company.

☐ Vary the activation offer made to your inactive accounts.

☐ Cease to send activation offers to your cardholders when they can no longer be profitably activated.

FREQUENT SHOPPER PROGRAMS

This is a new chapter in the revised edition of *Credit Card Marketing*. I have added it because of the enormous attention that frequent shopper and frequent buyer programs are getting in the mid-1990s. *Frequency programs,* as they are most often called, are discussed nearly every day in the executive offices of many banks, retailers, and T&E companies. They are trendy, exciting and, since some companies have jumped in, a necessary program for consideration to stay competitive.

Essentially, frequency programs reward your best credit card customers based on their total repeat business with your company. They take many forms and shapes, but all the recent ones were spawned by the airlines frequent flier programs introduced in the mid-1980s. They, in turn, got their idea from gas stations of the 1950s: When you bought gas, an attendant punched a card and after all the blocks on the card had been punched (8–10 fill-ups), you received a free set of glasses. Unfortunately, retailers or other businesses are not giving away empty seats on airplanes that fly daily from destination to destination anyway. As long as the airline industry does not sell out every seat on almost every flight, they have a real marketing success going. Lately, with lower ticket costs, more people are flying, and the airlines have begun to tighten up restrictions, qualifying award levels and mileage earned per flight.

My biggest challenge over the past few years has been to help evaluate the wisdom of frequent buyer programs for almost all retailers and for a few banks and other credit card companies. Many CEOs think a frequent buyer program is a panacea to hold onto their existing credit card customers or attract competitors' customers. I have no qualms with this rationale; however, frequent buyer programs are far more complicated than they appear to be at first blush. I have worked with, set up, or evaluated most of the frequent buyer programs throughout the United States.

CASE STUDY

While I have avoided discussion of specific companies in this book, Zayre (a discount retailer) is no longer in existence so I will describe the frequent buyer program they put in place in 1987. This example is not tied to a credit card program, but it illustrates the issues; we will cover credit cards themselves later in this chapter.

Zayre's introduced their program with a major advertising and marketing thrust that included lots of television, ROP advertising, flyers, and massive point-of-purchase signage in their stores. The television campaign featured a couple living it up on their free trip to some exotic Pacific island. A beautiful incentive gift catalog was produced full of hundreds of free prizes you could earn just by making your purchases at

Zayre. Each customer who filled out a form in the store received one of these full-color catalogs, which had a customer
ID number on it. These ID numbers had been preloaded into
Zayre's point-of-sale cash register systems. Every dollar you
spent in their store earned you 100 points.

This was the basic setup and structure of the Zayre program. Each time you made a purchase in their store, you gave
the cashier your ID number. The register receipt would display the number of points you had previously accrued, how
many points you earned with this purchase, and your new
grand total. Let's say you purchased $20 worth of miscella-
neous merchandise. That would earn you 2,000 points in the
frequent buyer program. Not bad. The average ticket at Zayre
about this time was less than $10. So every week, you would
come back in and buy your health and beauty supplies, paper
towels, blue jeans, and so on. In only a couple of months, you
would have accumulated 15,000 to 20,000 points ($150 to
$200 in purchases).

This appeared to be a pretty good deal—until you discovered that the lowest amount of points eligible for a free prize
was 35,000 to 50,000 for a coffee mug. That translates into
$350 to $500 in purchases. For a discount retailer with con-
sumables, health and beauty aids, and lower-end clothing,
that is a fair amount of purchases. So, customers soon figured out that to take that beautiful trip to the Pacific, they
would have to spend $150,000—the equivalent of buying two
or three of virtually every single one of the 15,000 items that
the store carried.

ANALYZE YOUR CUSTOMERS' NEEDS

This study case highlights the first essential you need to address. There has to be some realistic level of participation

that makes consumers believe they can get a worthwhile reward for channeling all their purchases to a specific retailer or a specific credit card. For years, Citibank issued CitiDollars for purchases made with their Visa cards. On the surface, accumulating those incentive dollars for using that particular Visa looked good to customers. The company put out a small catalog and regular inserts showing many items that could be purchased for reduced prices by applying a certain amount of CitiDollars. A television set, purportedly with a regular price of $199, could be purchased for $179 and $20 in CitiDollars. While some customers did perceive a value for this reduction in price, today's discount retail environment makes it hard to tell whether that television was a clear-cut value. And Citibank has now discontinued the CitiDollar program. I am not against frequency plans but am trying to stress how thoroughly you need to investigate the ramifications before getting involved in such programs.

ADMINISTRATIVE COSTS

To continue with the Zayre example, let's look at the retailer, bank, or T&E side of this equation. Any frequency program is difficult to administer. There is a massive issue with your computer systems. You will need to capture, track, and report the points or dollars that your customers earn. This can involve extensive programming, point-of-sale equipment, additional storage capacity within your systems, and a set of operating procedures for your operations center. Extra customer service representatives must be available to answer questions, process requests for awards, and adjust errors in customers points or dollars earned. If the customers get merchandise, fullfillments will need to be processed. You can do it the hard way (yourself), or numerous fullfillment businesses are available for this service. Several turnkey vendors provide the gift selections, fullfillment, tracking, and marketing guidance. All of the preceding requirements have associated costs that you must consider when looking into a frequency program.

MARKETING AND ADVERTISING COSTS

Next, you have the marketing costs. Your frequent buyer program is worthless if customers or potential customers are unaware of it. Attracting customers is the reason you are developing this program to begin with. At Zayre, they spent well over a million dollars to introduce and market their frequent buyer program. Television spots, ROP newspaper ads, in-store signs, inserts into your monthly billing statements, and other similar types of advertising and marketing efforts are part of making your program effective.

This cost will vary greatly depending on the amount of support you put behind your marketing plan. Discover Card invested heavily in print and television exposure for 1% cashback incentive, a plan that pays customers 1% back for all purchases each year. This frequent buyer program, (which introduced the Discover card) was the first to bring the cash rebate to the market and was certainly good positioning for the debut of a major new credit card. Remember though that 1% of $1,000 worth of annual purchases on a credit card represents only $10 to the customer.

AWARD COSTS

Then there is the cost of the service or merchandise that the customer receives free or at a greatly reduced price. Free to the customer is not free to the company. Zayre's coffee mug for 35,000 points meant that the customer had purchased $350 in merchandise. The cost of the mug was $3.50, which is a 1% cost-to-sales for the merchandise being given away. A few factors always affect this redemption cost. Most of the time, customers will need to accumulate their points over time which means your company's bottom line is not immediately hit with this cost; however, you will most likely want to accrue for it anyway. Another major factor is that not all customers will redeem their points. The ratios vary greatly from program to program, but an 80% redemption is probably on the high side. This means that ultimately, your merchandise costs at Zayre would be 0.8% cost-to-sales.

The greatest challenge with a frequent buyer program is keeping the bottom line cost-to-sales of the incentive within an acceptable range so as not to destroy or damage net before-tax profits. To do this, you must have an incentive that entices your customers to make the majority of their purchases with your company but that does not seriously impact your company's gross margin. In the Zayre example, even a cost-to-sales of less than 1% may have been too expensive for the company, while the required level of purchases was too high for customers to achieve. In essence, both the customers and the company had an unsatisfactory result.

PLAN CAREFULLY

Working with numerous banks and retailers, I have seen many versions of frequent buyer programs come and go. That volitility is another issue you should be aware of before starting your program. It is always easier to give something to your customers than it is to take away something they have been receiving from you. So, take care to think through any frequent buyer program over the long haul. You could risk losing customers by quickly starting up a program and shutting it down shortly thereafter. Customers would be offended that they did not have time to earn certain awards, and the fallout could be devastating to your company's sales. Also, redemptions will skyrocket when you shut down a frequent buyer program. One particular home center chain tried a program in the mid-1980s for about two years. Customers earned points by making purchases on the private label credit card program. The company used most of the marketing programs discussed in the preceding sections. At the end of the two years, management decided the program was just too expensive to keep. They sent notifications to all of their credit card base that they would be discontinuing the frequent buyer program, and redemption rates quadrupled. When the final score was tallied, the grand total cost of sales for the two-year period was nearly 9%. No retailer in the United States today can afford that kind of bottom-line cost.

Free merchandise is not the only type of reward customers can receive. One of the largest retailers in the country gives gift certificates based on levels of purchases. Customers can earn free gift wrap, additional discounts, or other less costly awards.

T&E credit cards and banks have come up with dozens of approaches to lure their credit card customers into concentrating their purchases on their card instead of several different credit cards or a competitor's card. You have no doubt been exposed to some of the following:

- The 1% cash-back program.
- Free airline miles on certain affinity Visa or Master-Cards.
- Buyer protection programs to cover your purchases.
- Free in-flight insurance.

- Tie-ins with car rental companies (that have their own frequent renters program).

- Tie-ins with hotels (that have their own frequent guests programs).

- Free gas on oil company credit cards.

- Annuities or savings bonds at certain levels of performance.

Banks have the same problems as retailers in limiting the costs associated with these incentives. After all, the free airline miles may be free to the airline, but they are not free to the bank that issues a credit card and offers the travel discount as an incentive. I find it novel that the airline companies actually found a way to offset some of the no-rev (nonrevenue) customers they have as a result of their frequent flier program by getting banks and retailers to partner-up and share some of the expense. And yet, all of us have to be competitive. If one bank, retailer, or T&E credit card company offers an incentive for customers to use its own credit card, the rest of the industry cannot sit by and let that firm gobble up market share.

SUMMARY

When added together, systems costs, marketing costs, and the cost of the incentive can represent a rather formidable price to put a frequent buyer program in place. Ironically, while you can almost exactly predict the cost of all the various components, it is much harder to predict the incremental sales increase you need or expect. We all know just how difficult it is to determine that a particular customer made a particular purchase as a result of the frequent buyer program. Generally, all we know is that we had an overall increase in sales, or spike, during the promotion. The increased sales may be attributable to several things, but usually the spike is obvious enough to credit a large portion to your program. Even if your system can track specific customers, it is still difficult to tell whether you are getting any lift from your frequency program after the first year or two.

A Canadian retailer has had a frequent buyer program for several years now and is often cited as the success story to look at when frequency companies meet with retailers. At first, that retailer did have a nice lift in sales, but now it is hard to tell whether any additional lift is coming from the program. In addition, the costs have now settled in and are somewhat higher than expected.

I am not suggesting that you cannot develop a successful frequent buyer program, only that to do so cost-effectively and with enough incremental sales increases requires a tremendous amount of research, planning, and forethought.

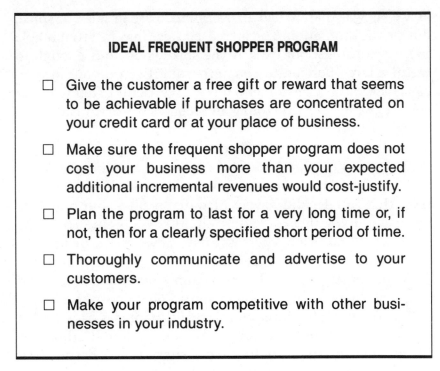

IDEAL FREQUENT SHOPPER PROGRAM

☐ Give the customer a free gift or reward that seems to be achievable if purchases are concentrated on your credit card or at your place of business.

☐ Make sure the frequent shopper program does not cost your business more than your expected additional incremental revenues would cost-justify.

☐ Plan the program to last for a very long time or, if not, then for a clearly specified short period of time.

☐ Thoroughly communicate and advertise to your customers.

☐ Make your program competitive with other businesses in your industry.

CREDIT CARD REISSUE

From time to time, credit card issuers may reissue their credit cards. Banks and T&E companies tend to reissue credit cards every one to three years. Most retailers and oil companies rarely reissue although there is a very recent trend in this direction.

With banks and T&E companies, the reissue is driven mostly by the need to control losses, delinquencies, and fraud. Cost of the reissue is covered within the annual fee (if there is one) and by savings from fewer written-off accounts.

On the other hand, retailers and oil companies tend to reissue only if they have to for reasons such as the following:

- Buyout of another company or credit card portfolio.
- Change of image or logo.
- Change in service provider (third party).
- Technological requirements (changing to a mag stripe card).

My experience has been that a card reissue, for any reason, represents another marketing opportunity.

BENEFITS OF REISSUING CARDS

For retail and oil credit cards, the opportunity to increase activation rates and increase sales is enormous. More recently, banks have discovered this powerful opportunity. Many banks now offer value-added services such as credit card registration with their card reissue as well as other banking services such as CDs, savings plans, or mutual fund services. To date, I have not seen a credit card reissue that did not create a noticeable sales impact, especially if it included an incentive to come in and use the "new credit card." Often, the sales generated are the largest of all credit promotions.

Just think, this is probably the only time that you may send a direct mail piece to your entire credit card base. As covered in Chapters 9 and 16, it is usually best to segment your card base for sales promotions, which means you will rarely, if ever, send every single cardholder a promotion. However, since you have to mail all your credit card customers a new card when you reissue, you may as well use this opportunity to turn it into a powerful marketing and promotional program.

Promotions that ride along with a new credit card usually outperform normal promotions. The only explanation I have found over numerous card reissues with a large variety of retailers and banks is that consumers seldom carry all the credit cards they own. Survey questions have shown a trend over the past several years for more and more consumers to carry only frequently used cards. My guess is that consumers forget about or misplace some of those credit cards stored at home. When they get a brand-new reissue, along with a sales promotion, they now have a new credit card in their hands and simultaneously a reason to use it.

Compelling offers that ride along with reissued cards tend to have results ranging from a few percentage points to as much as 50% better than your usual promotional efforts.

On top of the enormous sales opportunity, your costs for the promotion are probably much lower than your average credit sales promotion because your activation sales offer rides along postage-free as a letter or insert within the credit card reissue. You could even eliminate the letter or insert cost by using the bottom panel of your credit card carrier as a tear-off coupon. After all, you have to mail the credit card (first-class postage) and a reissue goes out to your entire credit card base (usually) including all active and inactive accounts.

With 100% savings on postage, you greatly reduce the normal cost of any targeted promotional effort.

Another opportunity often overlooked in a credit card reissue is the benefit of using the nonforwarding postal regulation with first-class postage. The returned mail is usually only used by your collection department or processing center; however, this is one more place to flag customers in your direct marketing database.

Even if you do not reissue your entire credit card base for any of the preceding reasons, you undoubtedly issue replacement cards for those that are worn out or lost and stolen. Think of the response to an offer of credit card protection insurance if it is included with the replacement card you send to a customer who has just had a card lost or stolen. Come up with year-round promotions that you can send with all replacement cards. Only a very few companies have caught on to this cost-effective and highly successful way to promote sales and services.

In summary, don't overlook an extraordinary opportunity to increase your sales or services when you perform any credit card reissue.

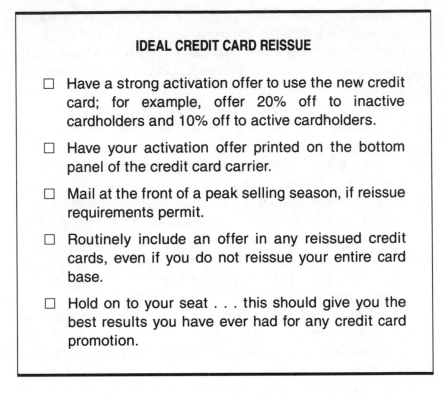

IDEAL CREDIT CARD REISSUE

☐ Have a strong activation offer to use the new credit card; for example, offer 20% off to inactive cardholders and 10% off to active cardholders.

☐ Have your activation offer printed on the bottom panel of the credit card carrier.

☐ Mail at the front of a peak selling season, if reissue requirements permit.

☐ Routinely include an offer in any reissued credit cards, even if you do not reissue your entire card base.

☐ Hold on to your seat . . . this should give you the best results you have ever had for any credit card promotion.

CARD ENHANCEMENT PROGRAMS

Card enhancement programs add value to your credit card and in most instances create additional sources of income from your credit card base. Most often, these offers are sent to your credit card customers as inserts into their monthly billing. Sometimes, bangtail payment envelopes are used. "Bangtail" is the terminology used for the envelope with an extra flap on the return side, which usually carries a marketing offer or change of address information. On rare occasions, a direct solo mail offer may be used, but the economics of enhancement programs usually prevent this option because of the additional postage cost. Response rates are usually similar to catalog or direct mail offers. Your response rate may run from as low as a few basis points to as high as a few percentage points. Response rates will vary depending on the offer you use and the strength of your own credit card customer base. Banks, retailers, and T&E credit card bases generally have similar response rates.

Far too often, companies summarily dismiss these programs because they do not understand them or do not know how to position these opportunities within the company or with customers. Comments heard over the years include, "We don't sell those types of items . . . our customers are not interested in any of those services . . . we don't want to clutter up our billing statement . . . we tried one of those years ago . . . it's too much trouble."

Nevertheless, if planned properly, executed consistently, and backed by reputable service providers, credit card enhancement programs can be very beneficial to your customer base and add plus net profits to your bottom line.

Examples of Enhancement Programs

Enhancements include the following:

1. Credit card registration.
2. Credit insurance.
3. Merchandise offers.
4. Continuity programs (programs that repeat):
   - Book series.
   - Legal plans.
   - Date minder services.
   - Credit report monitoring.
   - Auto clubs.
   - Buying services.
5. Educational offers.
6. Additional insurance options:
   - Life insurance.
   - Accidental death insurance.
   - Health insurance.
   - Renters insurance.
   - Credit card account insurance.

As you can see, there are lots of options. Selectively, such offers are good for your credit card program because cardholders perceive them as another benefit of owning and using your credit card. They give your credit card more utility and a broader range of benefits.

There are several major considerations:

- First, decide whether the enhancement program under consideration provides a benefit for your customers. For example, "Is credit card registration a good service to offer our customers through our credit card program?" If the product or service does not benefit your customers, then don't pursue it.

- If the answer to the preceding question is yes, then the second question is, "Will the vendor/partner for my credit card registration program provide as good customer service as I would?" Closely related to this is the stability of the vendor/partner. You must feel sure that the vendor/partner's company will be in business to provide the products or services you will be using.

- If the answer to the preceding question is yes, then the final question is "How much additional revenues can this type of program add to my bottom line?"

HOW TO USE ENHANCEMENTS TO INCREASE REVENUE

Over the years, I have used many of these programs—everything from pocket watches, coin sets, credit card registration, the first prepaid legal plan, encyclopedias, to workout videotapes. In most cases, these and other products and services have proven to be good for our credit card customers and good for our bottom line.

Banks have an opportunity here to expand beyond the basic financial services, and oil companies have the chance to broaden their product offers.

There are usually two main ways to generate revenues from credit card enhancement programs:

1. Many banks and oil companies alike prefer a straight per thousand inserted revenue, such as $10 or $20 per thousand inserts placed within their billing statements regardless of the response rates or resulting sales. This is a predictable way to determine your profit up front and lock in a specific dollar amount of revenue.

2. Many retailers prefer a commission basis where they get 15% to 30% of the gross or net revenues generated from the sales of the products or services offered. If you take this approach, you are sharing in the risk of the success or failure of a particular insert, and the card enhancement vendor/partner may offer you a larger share of the revenues generated. There is obviously a downside to this option, but there is also an upside. Should you hit a grand slam home run with a particular insert, your profit potential will greatly exceed any per thousand rate that you would have been able to guarantee up front. Over the years, my tendency has been to take the second approach because of the opportunity for much greater revenues. After all, vendor/partners are not likely to suggest any product or service they think will be a loser.

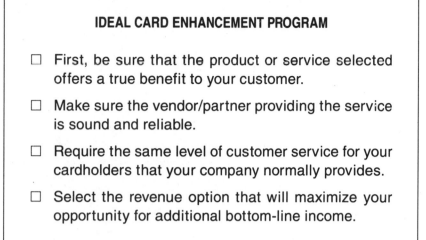

IDEAL CARD ENHANCEMENT PROGRAM

☐ First, be sure that the product or service selected offers a true benefit to your customer.

☐ Make sure the vendor/partner providing the service is sound and reliable.

☐ Require the same level of customer service for your cardholders that your company normally provides.

☐ Select the revenue option that will maximize your opportunity for additional bottom-line income.

GOLD CARDS, VIP,
AND PLATINUM CARDS

The 1990s have brought an explosion of segmentation of credit card customers within the existing card base. As more and more banks, retailers, and T&E companies have discovered the power in database marketing, they are exploring possibilities within the credit card base of customers they already have. We have looked for ways to leverage the investment already in our credit card base as well as ways to apply this knowledge to new account acquisition.

A few years ago, the first test was run to see how customers would react to the positioning of a status card. You may recall when owning an American Express or Carte Blanche card was perceived to be something better than average. A little elite, if you will, a status symbol that seemingly meant you were a cut above the average person. Ironically, it took several years for the banks to catch on and even several more years for retailers to recognize the value of applying this marketing approach.

Do you have an American Express regular (green) card, gold card, or platinum card? You pay for the privilege of having any of these cards and you pay more for each level. Only 10 years ago, no bankcard or retailer charged you to own its credit card. It is probably safe to say that most banks feared the loss of customers if they charged for their card. So why would you pay to own an American Express, further still, pay substantially more to own a platinum card?

Although you gain some additional benefits for each level of card, most of the appeal (as studies have shown) has to do with status and ego. There is a certain amount of pride when you present your platinum American Express to pay for a purchase. You feel as if you are in a very select group and that this card represents a certain status symbol.

Banks broke the ice and went to annual fees when Jimmy Carter put controls on credit and interest and essentially caused many of us to do things in the credit industry that we would never have done otherwise. We raised annual percentage rates and started charging annual fees, late fees, and minimum fees. We raised our credit standards and approved fewer accounts, all aimed at trying to survive when the entire economy was collapsing around us. And to our surprise, many consumers paid us. With this general background as a starting point, look at what has now happened within our credit card programs.

BENEFITS OF GOLD CARDS

Virtually all MasterCard and Visa banks have regular and gold cards. The marketing and advertising campaigns behind the gold cards position the card as a status symbol.

In addition, dozens of retailers have now entered the arena with their own tiered cards. Regular accounts for (I guess) regular customers, gold cards, platinum cards, president's club cards, chairman's club cards, and so on. Many surveys and studies have concluded that when your best customers are issued a higher-level card, their purchases go up. I have been involved in tests where credit card customers for a particular retailer were divided into several groups: Customers in the first group kept their regular retail credit card; the second group received a gold retail card with no additional features or benefits; the third group received a regular retail card with extra features and benefits; and the fourth group received a gold retail card with extra features and benefits. The gold card groups outperformed the regular groups in every test. So it is quite obvious that the higher the status symbol can be perceived, the better your resulting sales will be.

By offering benefits to your best customers and giving them recognition as VIPs or special customers, you will almost certainly continue to see increases in the loyalty and sales results from them. In today's target-marketed, database age, some retailers have found that you can keep segmenting the file and continue to increase your sales. To this end, some retailers have three or four levels of consumer credit cards: a regular credit card, then a gold card with one or two benefits such as free parking, then a platinum card with a few better benefits such as free gift wrap, then a president's card with even more benefits.

In segmenting credit cards, you have to be aware of the types of benefits you make available to each higher level of cardholder. After customers have graced you with purchases all year long because you issued them a gold retail credit card that allows them to park free and get free gift wrapping, these elite cardholders tend to say, "Now, what are you going to do for me?" You must plan ahead to be sure you don't increase benefits from year to year to the point that you begin to exceed the incremental benefits with incremental costs. These are not short-term programs. You need to plan carefully since the worst thing you could do is give your best customers a gold card with extra benefits and then take it away from them.

IDEAL GOLD CARD PROGRAM

☐ Give a perception of high status to your best cardholders.

☐ Include extra benefits or services for this group of customers.

☐ Plan a long-term program.

☐ Make sure a gold card will add incremental sales and profits to your company's bottom line.

☐ Make sure you are competing effectively with other gold card programs in your industry.

PART III

TRAINING EMPLOYEES TO MARKET CREDIT CARDS

TRAINING

There is no such thing as too much training. Another good title for this chapter would be "Communication." You simply cannot overtrain or overcommunicate your credit card program to your employees.

Unlike the 1970s and early 1980s when customers would literally seek you out and ask you for your company's credit card, you now have to seek customers out and sell them on why they should carry your credit card instead of, or in addition to, your competitor's credit card.

Were you to have the ideal set of circumstances (and some companies do), your credit card program would be a part of your company's orientation procedure for new employees on their first day at work. I am not referring here to standard operational training but to the provision of training on account acquisition—how to tell customers about the benefits of owning the credit card—and the importance of the credit card program to your company. Promoting your credit card program should be a requirement, not an option, for employees. In the most successful companies, fostering the credit card program is an everyday part of the employee's job, just as waiting on a customer or ringing up a sale is a routine part of the daily job. This corporate attitude must start at the top of your company with the president and CEO.

Various companies use literally dozens of methods and approaches. Some companies require each employee to get two applications per 40 hours worked. Some companies tie their store manager's bonuses, in part, to the number of credit card accounts opened at the store during the year. Some companies provide permanent spiffs (commissions) or contest monies for each account opened.

Unfortunately, other companies simply ignore the importance of their credit card program and only tell their employees about the credit card sporadically (or not at all) leaving the employees to fend for themselves, learning by trial and error (or not at all). As with most programs, the best approach is a consistent year-round focus on your credit card program with occasional extra contests or incentives to create extra excitement or introduce new features or benefits.

TRAINING AND EDUCATION GUIDELINES

Regardless of your approach, you must address several critical training and communication issues to have an optimally successful credit card program. The following sections describe these guidelines.

Make Credit Card Training a Standard Procedure

Include your credit card program as a standard part of the initial training that new employees receive when they first come to work. Some companies use manuals, some offer field training classes, and some use videotapes or audiocassettes. The training we are talking about here goes beyond operational routines. In most instances, when retailers or banks have an extensive ongoing training program for their employees, it focuses on operational training. They train employees how to process a credit card or a new application, correct an error, authorize sales, balance each day's credit card business, and address customer questions about billing or payment problems.

The credit card training I am discussing here should explain how to approach every customer with a request to apply for or use your credit card. It should address how to overcome objections and how to communicate the special benefits that customers receive. It should stress the importance of your credit card program to the company. Your training should cover important marketing features of your credit card such as a low APR or interest-free options.

In today's tough competitive environment, where most businesses now understand the vital importance of credit cards to their business, your employees need training in how to sell your credit card program. You want your associate to mention the credit card program early in the conversation with a customer. Likewise, the last thing the salesperson says when the customer is about to pay for the purchase is "Will this be on your XYZ account?" In this way, your employee has completed the loop from making a customer aware that you offer credit, should the person need it, to reminding the customer at the point of sale that you have your own credit card program.

Just as you give employees intensive training in product knowledge and customer service, and show them how to sell product features and benefits, they need the same knowledge base to sell customers on the reason they should apply for your company's credit card.

Establish Weekly and Monthly Goals

This will encourage continuity for your credit card program. It is always easier to achieve a higher level of performance if you have a goal to strive for. For maximum results, however, set low and easily achievable goals. Nothing is worse than a goal set so high that employees routinely dismiss it as impossible and never make the effort. You will always be better off if 90% of your employees perform at a consistent level than if 10% of your superstars produce the majority of your results.

Familiarize Employees with the Credit Card Center

Ideally, new employees should work at the credit card center for a day or two. This instills a sense of confidence about the people servicing the credit card operation and can establish rapport. Have you ever heard a sales associate or teller complain about "those people in the credit center" as though the center is another company? And even if it were another company, what difference should it make? The customer is in your store, purchasing your products from your employees with your credit card. Remarks like this tell me that the employees do not have enough knowledge or understanding of their own credit card program.

Recognize That Training Must Be an Ongoing Process

Turnover makes it inevitable that a few months after your training session, there will be several new employees on board who must be trained. Because of the enormous turnover prevalent in many companies these days, you are better off to have a short, easy-to-learn, and simply administered training program.

Lengthy, detailed training sessions may impart more information, but for the employees who stick with you, this extra knowledge will be obtained through on-the-job experience and the association with long-term employees. If you are too thorough or too complicated, you will simply lose the employees' interest, not to mention that a large percentage of these new employees will not be with you over the long haul.

Don't Limit Training to Store Employees

Employees in many areas within your corporate headquarters interact with the credit card department and also need to know about your credit card program. The advertising, marketing, store operations, and accounting departments will be touched by your credit card program constantly. The more they understand your credit card, the better they will support it.

A few years ago, an accounting manager spoke up at one of our operating meetings and said, "We really need to get rid of this credit card registration service we offer because we get covered up with cancellations all the time."

When I asked her how many cancellations per week or month, she estimated from 20 to as many as 100. I then informed her that we had a quarter-million customers enrolled and that this year the credit card registration service had generated nearly $500,000 of net revenue. She then realized that 10 to 100 cancellations represented a minor problem in light of the hundreds of thousands of customers using the service.

Include Your Credit Card Program in Regional and Management Meetings

In maintaining constant and ongoing communications, you need to be sure that your credit card is a part of managerial meetings. This allows you to share important positive information with the people in the field who work with your program every day, and its presence on the agenda underscores the importance of the credit card program.

Use the Credit Card for Name Tags

Adapt your actual credit card for use as the name tag that most employees wear. This is a professional way to keep the credit card in front of all your employees and customers and it promotes the credit card at the same time. It used to be a novel approach; however, over half the retailers in the United States now use this technique.

KEEP EMPLOYEES INFORMED BY COMMUNICATING OFTEN

Far too often, companies communicate important credit card program information through infrequent, but voluminous, memos or manuals. That may be OK, but it is not the best answer. Do you really believe that every employee enthusiastically grabs a 15-page memo about your credit card program and with gleeful expectation soaks in every single word without even laying it aside for even a moment? Probably not! Would you?

Do you really believe that one copy of an important credit card memo posted on a bulletin board or passed around the store really reaches all 150 employees within the store?

What is your turnover? If it is 50%, then 5% of your employees change every 2 weeks. Who kept the copy of that really important credit card memo from last week and diligently gave it to the newest employee who started today?

In addition to the problems created by the method and regularity of communications, 15 other departments are trying to get your employees' attention at the same time. For all these reasons and others, you cannot overcommunicate.

There are many ways to combat this communication problem:

- Use audiocassettes to announce contests or important credit card program changes or details. They are very inexpensive, require no reading, and communicate the same message equally to everyone. Appendix B lists a company that can provide these cassettes.

- Keep your written memos and other written communications short. I once sent a memo to 300 stores that only had one word on it. It really got some attention!

- Be different. When you send your memos, use colored paper or print them upside down.

- Recruit others to help you communicate. Pass important messages along to regional managers, district managers, or others who will help get the word out.

- Attend every meeting you can or at least have someone include the credit card program in every meeting possible.

- Have your own credit card newsletter or at least be represented in every issue of your company's newsletter.

- If your budget permits, use videotapes to communicate important events. The production cost is high, but the cost may sometimes be justified.

- Have your credit department call the key managers directly if you have a really important message to get out.

- Periodically, survey your own store employees to get their feedback and input. This allows you not only to learn about areas for improvement but also to communicate new products or services.

IDEAL TRAINING PROGRAM

☐ Make training regular and ongoing—a never-ending process.

☐ In corporate credit card training into your company's overall training program.

☐ Use many methods to communicate messages such as audiocassettes, meetings, videotapes, and unusual memos.

☐ Make the credit card program a part of the job description for all new employees.

☐ Tie the field/store management incentive compensation to specific goals.

Employee Contests

This is one of my favorite marketing programs. Over the years, I have helped develop hundreds of employee contests, spiff (commission) programs, incentive plans, and employee recognition programs of all types. I am proud to have introduced the first employee contest in the nation that utilized the rub-off or mystery sale concept described later in this chapter. Since then, dozens of major retailers have used rub-off contest programs very successfully.

The purpose of a contest is to motivate the employees who are not performing at the level you want or need, not to reward the employees who do the best job. I know that this statement will be challenged by some, but think about it. Historically, about 10% of your employees do everything you ask and then some. They get the vast majority of the new account applications that you receive day in and day out. About 10% of your employees do very little of what you ask. They would not work to get credit card applications if you offered a

brand-new car as a reward. Therefore, about 80% of your employees—most of your staff—are the ones that you actually
can motivate to do a better job.

Employee contests and incentives have many advantages
and few disadvantages. For them to be consistently successful, however, you must pay great attention to the planning,
execution, and communication of the program. I have evaluated many employee contests that were successful and
some that failed. This chapter will give you guidelines for a
superior contest.

Most of the major retailers and banks I have worked with
are strong supporters of employee incentives. Occasionally,
though, a company executive will say, "We pay our employees to do their job now, and that should be sufficient." Now,
in an ideal world that may be a reasonable position, but in reality that is rarely the case. Some companies build into the
employee's job description a requirement for "x" amount of
credit applications per 40 hours or per 8 hours worked. These
are good ideas. To be consistent, the store manager should
have some type of credit application goal tied to his/her annual bonus compensation.

These operational goals, however, do not remove the need
to reward your employees, from time to time, for their extra
efforts in the area of credit card accounts, or any other company program you wish to emphasize.

Employee contests do not need to be expensive to work.
As a matter of fact, in one of the largest credit card programs
in the United States today (which I initiated and managed for
several years), the employee contest applications were the
least costly and most productive accounts we obtained while
building our program.

Employee contests are beneficial for several reasons:

- Contests reward your employees for effort above and beyond their day-to-day performance.

- Contests add a positive spin to what could otherwise be considered a difficult job requirement.

- Contests have the additional benefit of training. Employees who get involved because of the extra incentive will know more about the credit card program after the contest than they did before.

- Contests create an air of excitement that can move throughout your company and even your customers.

Although there are a number of pitfalls, an example later in this chapter shows how to avoid problems and run a successful contest.

Contests can be very simple such as a spiff paid to the employee for each application completed, or they can be very complicated, involving multiple options, drawings, and so on.

PLANNING AN EMPLOYEE CONTEST: GENERAL GUIDELINES

- **Start with a definite goal for your employee contest.** "All you can get" is not a goal. The goal should be reasonable and attainable by everyone involved. If you create too high a goal, thinking that the employees "should" be able to achieve it, they may choose not to get involved at all. Have you ever participated in a contest or incentive where, for one reason or another, you knew from the start who would win (One of the competitors has a bigger store or more customers. . . . We have never had that many credit applications since our store opened 25 years ago. . . . Joe is good at getting applications, and I will never be able to beat him)? See what I mean?

By setting the goal at a reasonable level, you will prevent most employees from eliminating themselves.

- **Count *all* the applications taken by employees, not just the approved ones.** Rarely have I seen an employee contest work where the responsibility of a customer's credit file has been put on the employee. It may sound OK, and most credit marketing managers feel it is the most cost-effective way to run a contest, but in reality it is full of negatives.

  What really happens is that two employees in the same store or bank each get five customers to apply for your credit card account. By the luck of the draw (credit file), one employee has four approved while the second employee has all five applications turned down. Now both employees put forth the same amount of effort, but one employee receives the reward. Even worse, one employee may take three applications and the other one five applications. If all three applicants are approved for the first employee and all five are declined for the second employee, then the first employee actually is rewarded for showing less effort.

  Another disturbing side effect is that declined applications may be challenged just because they negatively affect an employee's opportunity to be rewarded in the contest.

- **Do not run year-round spiffs or contests.** Some companies run their employee spiffs all the time. For example, a major department store chain pays a two-dollar commission for every credit card application taken. True, you do get a lift from paying the spiff. However, after a while, this extra money becomes just another part of the employees' regular income; it loses *its* power as an incentive. Watch your application flow and you will see that after the rise in volume when you introduce the spiff, it will level off, decline, and eventually may not be much higher than it was before you started. This is somewhat like last year's raise. It was great, but what do I get this year?

- **Run your spiffs or contests for short bursts, ideally six weeks in most cases.** Why six weeks? The contest doesn't always have to be six weeks, of course, but that length of time accomplishes a couple of things. Just because you start a credit application contest next Monday doesn't mean that all your employees know about it by then. In fact, it seems that it takes about two weeks for everyone to find out about such programs. There are a lot of reasons for this. Perhaps your store meetings are on Thursdays. Some of your store managers may be out on vacation, or sick, or were too busy to get around to the contest this week!

  Some managers may think this is an exaggeration— and it is in no way meant to be negative—it is just the way business operates in many instances. So, allow two weeks for the word to get around and everyone to get going in the contest. That leaves four weeks: time enough for the excitement to peak, time enough to send out the standings a couple of times, but not time enough for the excitement to fade out.

- **Be sure to include everyone in your contest.** Far too often, contests are run that reward only the store manager or branch manager. That sounds good, since he/she is the leader or manager of the team, but that will seldom motivate the front-line employees. After all, the managers already earn more than their employees.

  Sometimes, contests are run where the whole store wins the prize; a cookout, for example. Again, that's OK, but there may be quite a few employees who can't go to the cookout, don't want to go to the cookout, or do not feel that the reward is worth the effort required.

There are ways to include everyone and still stay within a reasonable budget. We will go over those in the sample contest at the end of this chapter.

- **Answer the question, "What's in it for me?"** If the employee feels the answer is "nothing," then that is the level of involvement you will get from the employee (except for those 10% who do their best all the time). For your employees to get really involved and get behind your credit card contest, they must have, or perceive they have, something to gain, individually! Let's say, for example, that your immediate supervisor comes into your office today and says, "Guess what? I have a chance to win a trip around the world and $10,000 in cash and all I need is for you to work twice as hard, get twice as many credit card applications, maybe three times as many as normal, and I'll be on my way."

  Now true, this person is your boss and you must respond to the requirements of your job, but do you honestly get excited about the trip your boss will get if you work twice as hard (maybe three times as hard)?

  Now let's throw just a slight twist into this situation. Your boss says, "And you'll get a $1,000 cash bonus." Wow!

- **Find innovative and exciting ways to announce your contest.** Many a well-planned, solid, dynamic, and lucrative contest has failed because the announcement of the contest was buried under reams of paperwork, manuals, or brochures that would take weeks to read, or because the only copy of the announcement was hung on the bulletin board in the break room.

  Even if you painstakingly produce what should be an extremely successful contest, it is all for naught if you don't get the word to the people you are trying to motivate. Here's another rule of thumb: "If the message you are trying to communicate cannot be grasped in less than five seconds, your message will not get across."

Five seconds may be too much. Let's all take a little test right now. Did you receive any mail or memos today? How long did you spend looking at them? Some of the mail you didn't even open. Why not? How long did it take you to decide whether to open it or trash it? What about your memos? Did you look first to see who sent them and then decide which ones to read? I bet you picked the 48-pager from your MIS department about an important programming change for your credit card program and read every word without stopping. As my 16-year-old son, Anthony, would say—*Not.*

See what I mean? Keep this need for brevity in mind when you put together the method for communicating your contest to all your stores.

Here are some suggestions for communicating your contest. I am an advocate of using all of them simultaneously:

1. **Contest Brochure.** Keep it short and sweet. For example, **WIN $1,000 INSTANTLY.** Your employees will find the details if they understand the reward.

2. **Audiocassette.** Professionally produced and copied, this can be an incredibly inexpensive way to deliver the same message to everyone and with lots of razzmatazz (see Appendix B for vendor/partner).

3. **Videotape.** Budget permitting, this is a better medium than the audiocassette.

4. **Announcement at a Manager's Meeting.** Or, choose any other meeting where you can inform many of the key employees about this fantastic contest.

5. **Electronic Messages.** Some companies have technological ways of communicating important information to their stores immediately. This is important.

6. **A Theme.** Tie your contest to something. One company used Batman as a theme for their contest; different characters from the movie became people at the corporate headquarters. The audiocassette had a lot of fast and exciting music.

7. **Premiums/Promotional Items.** Send other premiums with the contest brochure. This works especially well if you have used a supporting theme. For example, the company that used Batman sent Batman T-shirts to the stores for personnel to wear during the kickoff while they listened to the audiocassette.

8. **Publish Standings Regularly.** List all stores so they can compare how they are doing. (Always try to transmit copies through your company president or the vice president of store operations since the standings will also point out those who aren't with the program.)

9. **Have a Follow-Up Procedure.** Your staff should call each store as a follow-up to be sure they got the contest package and to answer any questions they may have. (This may be difficult if you have many stores.)

10. **Constantly Communicate Good Results.** If you have a store or two that make the goal in the first week, send out a special recognition to those stores. Equally important, let the rest of the stores know.

11. **Use the Mystery Shopper Technique.** Early in the contest, have a few people who are not known by your store personnel visit your store. If the sales associate who waits on them, asks them to apply for your credit card, they award the associate with cash on the spot.

The store manager should announce the winner, and the winners and winning stores should be publicized across the company.

These are just a few ideas; the point simply is that you cannot overcommunicate—although you can easily use too many words. The one-word memo I sent years ago to our field operations produced more calls and attention to that project than any of the voluminous memos we dispatched on a regular basis. Think about it!

PLANNING AN EMPLOYEE CONTEST: AN EXAMPLE

Now let's plan a contest. There are literally thousands of ways to structure successful contest programs, but the following example describes one of my favorite methods: a contest using the rub-off concept.

Always start with a budget or goal. Let's say that we usually spend about $3.00 per application as an employee spiff. To plan our contest, we will use an imaginary company with 100 stores in five 20-store districts. Each store processes an average number of 15 credit card applications weekly. The length of our contest is six weeks and we want to get 10,000 new applications during the contest.

Based on $3.00 per application times the goal of 10,000 new applications, our budget should be $30,000. If we divide 10,000 applications among 100 stores, we need an average of 100 applications per store. To determine if this is a realistic goal, we see how this figure compares with our actual experience. Dividing 100 per store by six weeks equals about 17 applications per week, and we know we normally receive 15 per week. This is reasonable. Remember to keep your goals lower rather than higher so as not to discourage the stores.

Our peak holiday selling season begins the day after Thanksgiving in November, so we will structure the contest to end about two weeks prior to this date. That way, we will have good store traffic, mail the approved credit cards prior to the peak season, and be through with our contest when the sales associates are busiest making sales. This means our contest should start October 1.

Let's pick a theme to use with our contest. How about "Credit Card Cash for the Holidays." When the contest begins, we can have some of Santa's elves (mystery shoppers) visit a few stores to give out instant cash if the salesperson asks them to complete a credit card application.

Now, who will earn cash or prizes?

- Store manager (1 per region).
- Assistant store manager (1 per region).
- Department manager.
- Sales associates.
- Warehouse personnel.
- Regional managers.
- Credit office or back office personnel.

Absolutely the most important person to start with is the sales associate.

We need a Grand Prize. In keeping with the Christmas theme, let's make that a $1,000 shopping spree.

How are we going to announce the contest and when? Here are a few ideas:

- Release the contest to the stores three working days before the starting date. This allows some time for the contest package to get there.
- Send an audiocassette, professionally produced (not longer than 5 minutes) to every store to be played at one or more store meetings.

- Create a contest brochure.
- Since there is a manager's meeting in September to prepare for the holiday season, announce an upcoming contest at that meeting. If it is within a week or so of our starting date, go ahead and hand out the contest package at that time.

By using the rub-off concept, we can manipulate the prizes under the rub-off to achieve our targeted goal within our alloted budget. But, *never have a losing game card!* Remember that we usually pay $3.00 for an application. We must never have less than $1.00 under the rub-off spot on the game card. That way, employees may not win a big prize, but they will never end up empty-handed either. An easy way to work out this part of the contest planning is to remember that you are working with $3.00 per application and break down all your costs on a per application basis.

Now let's put a couple of other cash or other prizes under the rub-off on our game cards. How about a $50.00 winner, a $25.00 winner, and four $5.00 winners? That means that in a pack of 100 game cards, six employees will win $95.00 and the other 94 get $1.00 each for a total of $189.00 or $1.89 for each application so far.

Now let's make all game cards eligible for a drawing for $1,000.00 in cash. Dividing the $1,000.00 by the goal of 10,000 applications, means we add 10 cents to our investment per application bringing us up to $1.99 each.

In most instances, the sales associate does not actually process the credit card application. Usually personnel in the credit office or back office perform this function. So, let's pay them 25 cents for every application processed in their store. If the store reaches 100 applications, they have earned an extra $25.00. Process 200 and they have earned $50.00. Add this 25 cents to our cost and we now stand at $2.24 per application.

The rest of the prizes will be based on the store as a whole making the team goal of 100. When the store achieves the team goal of 100 applications, the store manager will go into a drawing for $500.00 in cash and the assistant store manager will go into a drawing for $250.00 in cash, one entry for each 100 applications taken in their store. This adds 10 cents to bring our cost per application to $2.34.

For regional managers, the prize for averaging 100 applications per store for the 20 stores in their region is $200.00 in cash—no drawing. A sure $200.00 by averaging 100 applications per store in their district. Five regional managers means a total exposure of $1,000.00 or another 10 cents per application to bring our cost up to $2.44.

When each store achieves its goal of 100 applications, let's put all the rest of the employees in that store, who do not have an opportunity to ask customers to apply for a credit card account, into a drawing for $25.00 in cash. That's a winner in every single store (provided they achieve the team goal of 100). That brings our total up to $2.69 per application. Have you ever seen a warehouse person get involved in a credit card contest? They will sometimes ask the sales associates how many applications have been received, just to be sure the store makes the goal of 100. There are other ways to involve everyone, such as a free lunch for ineligible employees.

To run this contest, we need to produce the audiocassettes. For 100 stores, we will estimate $1,000.00 for production and duplication. We will also need to print about 15,000 of the rub-off game cards, which we estimate will cost $2,000.00. Let's throw in $100.00 for mystery shopper instant cash during the first day or two of the contest. Pick 10 stores at random. As an employee in each store asks you to apply, award them $10.00 on the spot. Then broadcast daily the winners so that all stores feel as though a mystery shopper may visit them. This additional $3,100.00 now brings our total cost to $3.00 per application, or $30,000.00, which was our original budget.

Had we been over budget at this point, we would simply go back through the cash prize distribution within each pack of 100 game cards and adjust accordingly. However, never have game cards with less than a $1.00 prize.

Now let's talk about how we promote this contest. On your contest cassette tape—with lots of up-beat, fast-paced music in the background—you announce, "Sales Associate, you could win up to $50.00 for just one credit card application and maybe even an extra $1,000.00 Grand Prize to boot. Simply ask your customer to complete our credit card application while in our store and win!"

Now, your contest gets a boost from management. Although the store managers and their assistants do not get something for each application, they have good odds of winning $500.00; even though they may not consider that a big incentive, it is enough to make them support your contest instead of ignoring it. And, guess what the regional managers do when they call or drop by their stores? They ask how many applications each store has taken. Why? Because they get a sure $200.00 for what they perceive as an easily attainable goal for every store.

About this time, a sales associate rushes to the office to get an application processed. The office manager or back office manager cheerfully says, "Great! Go get another one!" instead of, "Don't bring me any more credit applications today because I'm too busy."

Top this off with a mystery shopper who came through the store and gave four sales associates $25.00 each because they had asked the shopper to apply for a credit card account.

At the end of that week, a full recap of the standings by store arrives in each store's company mail sent directly from your president.

This type of contest fosters team spirit and excitement in all stores. You will always get more applications by having 100 stores promoting your program together than you will by

Exhibit 15-1
Sample employee contest announcement.

Win $1,000 SHOPPING SPREE and CASH

SALES ASSOCIATES: Win Up to **$50 Cash Instantly**

For every credit card application you take in your store, get an instant winner game card. You could win up to **$50** cash on the spot!

PLUS

Each game card entitles you to one entry in the grand prize drawing for **$1,000 SHOPPING SPREE** at the end of the contest.

STORE MANAGERS: Win **$500 CASH**

For each 100 applications taken in your store, you will receive one entry in a drawing for **$500 CASH.**

ASSISTANT STORE MANAGERS: Win **$250 CASH**

For each 100 applications taken in your store, you will receive one entry into a drawing for **$250 CASH.**

OFFICE MANAGERS: You get 25 cents for every application processed in your store—100 applications wins you **$25.**

ALL OTHER STORE PERSONNEL: Win **$25 CASH**

When your store reaches the team goal of 100 applications, your name will be placed in a drawing—one employee from each store wins **$25 CASH.**

REGIONAL MANAGERS: Win **$200 CASH**

If you average 100 applications per store for the stores in your region, you win **$200 CASH.**

having a half-dozen superstars. In addition, this balanced approach will keep your credit card program growing across your company and not just in a few key stores.

It would take a separate book to explore hundreds of novel ways to run successful employee contests that will motivate your employees. I hope however, that this example will get you started.

The sample contest brochure (Exhibit 15-1) shows you how to ensure that your message gets across to all those who need to receive it.

IDEAL EMPLOYEE CONTEST

☐ Have a clear goal that is within easy reach for all employees.

☐ Reward the employee for all applications taken, not just approved accounts.

☐ Do not run the contest year-round.

☐ Include everyone in the store and other regional management personnel who help supervise the stores.

☐ Always reward the individual sales associate who obtains a completed application.

☐ Make the contest exciting and announce it in a clear and enticing way.

PART IV

CREDIT CARD MARKETING TECHNIQUES

DATABASE MARKETING

80% of my revenue comes from 20% of my
customers. I just don't know who the 20% are.

~*Bill Grady*

As we entered the 1990s, it became increasing evident that
mass marketing was on the way out. The shotgun approach
no longer provided enough sales to offset the cost of creating
those sales. Printing costs were up, postage costs were up, and
response rates were down. Today, database marketing probably offers the largest single opportunity for retailers, banks,
and others to reduce cost and improve productivity. Because
of its importance, I have greatly expanded this chapter for the
revised edition of *Credit Card Marketing*, and I am planning
another book that will address only database marketing (what
I call *individual marketing*) and the opportunities it provides
for all types of advertising and promotions.

The shotgun approach is used frequently for credit card acquisition, reactivation, and credit sales promotions. When a credit card issuer has a sales promotion or activation program, all cardholders, active and inactive, may receive the promotion. When banks or retailers want to increase market penetration or establish a new market, their policy has been to mail to almost everyone in the market.

As the credit card base grows and response rates fall, we are being forced to reduce the number of promoted accounts. Our first decision is usually to promote only the active accounts or only the inactive accounts.

In today's environment, these general guidelines are no longer good enough. The most successful credit card issuers today have learned to target everything with precision. Targeting means selecting those credit card accounts that are most likely to respond to your promotion and would give you an acceptable profit or response.

At Service Merchandise, I put in place the first individual customer database system used by a major retailer. In the same way, you too must segment and analyze your own credit card base if you want to ensure your success.

To maximize your opportunity for tremendous sales increases and tremendous cost reductions simultaneously, you must be aware of three equally important and critical areas:

1. Capturing the information.
2. Maintaining the information.
3. Using the information.

If you do any one or two of the preceding tasks, but not all three, it will result in such ineffective performance that you will waste enormous resources and have less than optimum results.

In the late 1980s, the cost to build and maintain a database and to capture and store the necessary information was enormous. However, due to the rapidly exploding technological revolution, the cost of hardware, software, and storage has decreased tenfold by 1995 and continues to drop. For a few thousand dollars, you can now do with a personal computer and an incxpensive hard drive what took hundreds of thousands of dollars, mainframe, and high-tech support just a few years ago. As a matter of fact, the PC I am using to revise this book contains a database of 800,000 customers managed with fourth-dimension software.

We are not talking about just the billing maintenance of your credit card customer accounts or the general summarizing of piles of data. It's nice to know your average purchase, sales results from a promotion, and active or inactive accounts, but this general information is not sufficient to target individual customers, which is exactly what you are striving to do. There is a widely quoted saying to the effect that it is much easier and much more cost-effective to get the next sale from your last customer than it is to go find a new customer. I call it *mining your existing customers* to maximize the sales and profits from the investment you have already made in them.

When your great-grandparents shopped at the country store, the storekeeper knew them and they knew him. The storekeeper knew the whole family and remembered each child's name. He could recall what groceries Mom last bought and where; and he could pretty well tell when she would run out of sugar or coffee, or when Dad would need a new shirt or hat. The storekeeper also knew when Dad got paid and how he got paid. He accommodated that pay schedule by allowing the family to charge their goods until payday or until the crops came in.

During our industrial revolution in the United States and just after World War II, we began to depersonalize our retail and banking relationships. The population exploded and we all became numbers. Dozens and dozens of numbers for every conceivable function from our water bill to our banking services to our retirement planning. The "new" 1990s revolution of database marketing is our attempt to once again know our own customers on a personal, one-on-one basis.

During the 1980s, the development of software and the expansion of census data began to move the focus from mass marketing to direct marketing.

If you join the database revolution and apply sophisticated direct marketing technologies, you will not only know your customers on an individual basis, you will be in a position to project their future needs as well as your profit potential from every single one of them, individually. One industry segment—mail order—got a head start but all of us in banking and retail can now see the tremendous benefits from the proper application of individual marketing techniques.

SEGMENTING YOUR CUSTOMER BASE

Let's look at how this process works. Say your entire credit card base is 500,000 accounts. Of these, 200,000 owe a balance and 300,000 do not owe a balance. Here are some basic things to look for. Within the 200,000 accounts with a balance are all sorts of customers. Some customers who have not purchased for some time, perhaps even over a year, still owe a balance because they have not yet paid off their account from those past purchases. If you design a sales promotion aimed at active accounts and include this type of customer, then you are actually reaching someone who is not purchase active. On the other hand, other customers may have purchased many times this year but don't happen to owe a balance this month because they generally pay off their balance each month.

The point here is to start looking at your credit card base by segmenting it into categories. Most ideal would be to build a profitability model to apply to the categories. However, for now we will stay relatively basic. What you want to do is to start looking for the best combination of customer behaviors or results that will give you the highest return for the least promotional expense.

A favorite simile that I repeat to various major retailers is, "When your only marketing efforts are to insert flyers and run sales promotions to everybody, it's like flying over your markets and throwing your offers out of airplanes. Sure some of them may land in the yards of consumers who will buy, but it's not very cost-effective." In today's environment, this certainly applies to your credit marketing efforts.

By dividing your credit card base into segments based on the same recency, frequency, and monetary value used in direct marketing, you are able to better target your most profitable cardholders. This process requires much more than just the mechanics of compiling data.

The success of your segmentation involves the collection of the data, maintenance of the data, accuracy of the data, and the evaluation of the data. Having enormous amounts of data available and not using it or not knowing how to use it will only cost you money. The experience that you gain each time you manipulate your information and perform various promotions will be invaluable to your company.

Just think of the impact you will have on your company's profitability when you can reduce marketing cost while simultaneously increasing sales. Experience has taught me that a small percentage of your customers represent a very large percentage of your company's sales and profits.

A properly designed database system will provide additional and meaningful marketing help to banks and retailers with the following services or skills:

1. Evaluate the effectiveness of all promotions *on a customer-by-customer basis.*

2. Determine which customers can be profitably promoted and which customers would *not* respond profitably, market by market.

3. Define those areas where potential additional (profitable) customers could be effectively and profitably obtained.

4. Define the size and limits of each retail market (around each selling unit, or group of stores in a metro area).

5. Provide meaningful and easy ways to work with information to permit accurate comparisons of each market (i.e., compare the "home" zip plus the surrounding zips of *each* selling unit, or the metro area).

6. Provide valuable information to assist in determining where future store expansion is required, justified, and desirable.

7. Provide a "pool" of potentially active and valuable credit card customers. (By knowing the buying patterns of each customer, you can uniquely promote those who are making purchases with cash or other credit cards.)

Although there is not enough space here to get into the details of developing this type of system, let's look at how you could begin evaluating your credit card customers.

ANALYZING YOUR CUSTOMER BASE

The basic starting point is understanding recency, frequency, and monetary value and how these impact your bottom line. Recency refers to the last time that a customer made a purchase. Frequency tells you how often your credit card customer shops with you. Monetary value is the amount of goods or services purchased.

A cardholder shops eight times with you during the year. That would identify the shopper as up to eight times better than a cardholder who shopped only once. This is referred to as frequency. At the same time, another cardholder may shop only once but purchase 10 times your average purchase on that one shopping trip. This is referred to as monetary value. A third cardholder has made two purchases of your average purchase amount in the last 30 days. This is referred to as recency. These three examples represent the recency, frequency, monetary value formula mentioned earlier. These are some of the basic building blocks of information that will start you toward the process of database marketing.

As you compile these histories on your cardholders you will begin to segregate your entire card base into categories. Information at the individual customer level must be captured and managed over a period of time. The more historical customer data you accumulate, the better your segmentation will be. Likewise, the more detailed the data captured, the more potential for forcasting future needs of your customers. The goal is to have sufficient data that you build a one-on-one dialogue with each customer. You could assign values to each category and cross-reference all groups to get the best combination. The powerful marketing tool you gain is the ability to know the difference between cardholders. This enables you to concentrate your marketing dollars where you will get the best return.

The following paragraphs describe some of the ways you can look at combinations of RFM (recency, frequency, monetary value).

A customer comes into your store and purchases an item for $1,000 that represents her only visit to your store this year and her only purchase. A second customer makes a purchase of $75, but it is his tenth trip to your store this year. Yet a third customer made a $195 purchase yesterday. Which customer is the best one for your company? In the past, most marketing managers would jump at the $1,000 customer, but that may be a complete miss, since any efforts you make toward marketing to such customers may not bring them back ever again. A customer who has shopped 10 times is great, but is that as good as one who just bought yesterday?

Don't let this confuse you. Start by dividing your customers into groups; then you can begin to segment and cross-select the characteristics you want.

Let's say you divide your customers into 10 groups. The top 10% would be those customers who spent the most (monetary value) in a 6-, 12-, or 18-month period. You would quickly see that the top 20% to 30% of your card base purchased 60% to 80% of the total purchases of your entire card base. Now divide your card base into 10 groups based on number of purchases (frequency). Once again, the top two or three groups will represent the vast majority of your total sales and last, select a targeted period of time, such as the last six months (recency).

With this segmentation in hand, you can begin to set the parameters you prefer for a specific sales activation promotion. You may select the top 10% of dollars purchased the last six months, with a minimum of three purchases. What you will find is that a very small (10%) group of customers may represent over half your entire sales. When you send your sales promotion to this group, your response rate will be dramatically higher than when it goes out to all your card base in general; and the purchased amounts will be way above your averages.

Even if your total gross sales are slightly lower than if you had sent your promotion to the entire card base, your costs will have been 90% less to send this group your promotion. Many times, if you have properly selected your targeted customers for a promotion, you can exceed your sales goal and spend a lot less marketing dollars.

There is much more to this process, but this gives you a general overview. Remember, I said there were three equally important parts to developing and maximizing any database program. Let's look at each one in a little more detail.

1. **Capturing the Data.** What data do you capture? Simply, only data that you will use. If you are going to use SKU (stock-keeping units), then capture them. If you are going to use payment type or phone number, then capture it. If not, then you are wasting valuable time and building enormous files for nothing. In other words, if department level is sufficient for the merchandise purchased (such as clocks) and the exact clock purchased is not needed, then do not capture SKU level. But, whatever data you capture, capture as near 100% of that data as you can. You will not be able to achieve the targeting and efficiencies you need with incomplete or inaccurate data.

2. **Maintaining the Data.** You must keep your data accurate, up-to-date, clean, and free of garbage. Duplicate accounts, wrong addresses, incomplete customer names, partial sales history will all destroy the integrity of your entire database system. Once it is unreliable, the system is useless. You must go to great lengths to keep the addresses accurate and current, to verify the customer names and gender are complete, and to maintain only one file per customer or cardholder by carefully using sever merge-purge and de-dupe processes. Your system must follow customers as they move from city to city, get married or divorced, change business phones, or have children or other lifestyle changes.

    If you capture the correct data properly and then do not maintain its integrity, it is worthless.

3. **Knowing How to Use the Data.** It has been my fortune or mis-fortune to see many calamities as banks and retailers rush to get into database marketing. Managers at one company I worked with in Texas bragged that they had captured every single customer's name and address and every single piece of sales and transaction data involved in every single sale for nearly three years.

In looking at their advertising promotional plans, I saw only one program that called for any direct mail. All the rest of their promotions were through newspaper inserts into Sunday newspapers. I asked whether the one direct mail promotion was sent to this marvelous list of customers they had built and was told no, it went to a rented list.

So I asked, "Then, why are you putting your customers and your employees to the task of gathering all this information if you have no plans to use it?" The president and vice president of marketing looked at each other and became visibly upset that they had not recognized the gold mine they possessed, worse still that they had never used it.

Yet another company in Canada had similar access to all the data they could possibly want, but there was so much data and it was so cumbersome to sort through that they had trouble determining how to use it.

And one last example, a very large Fortune 100 company captured the data that could literally save the firm millions of dollars, used it as a one-time mailing list, and discarded it. Only to recapture it all over again, use it one time then discard it.

If you need a test to sway the skeptics in your company, perhaps even yourself, just find a way to segregate any one of the three standard measurements on a small group of your customers: recency, frequency, or monetary value. Slice off the top 30%, using any cut you want to make, and test that group in a marketing promotion against any of your normal mass marketing programs. It takes only one test. That is why our country's retailers and banks are rediscovering the power of one-on-one customer database marketing.

When you have captured data on your customers as we have outlined in this chapter, you can also apply the cost of goods sold and rank your customers by profitability. So going back to the first examples of three customers, if the person who made a $1,000 purchase one time bought a low-margin (5%) product on sale in her isolated visit, how does she compare with the customer who purchased $195 yesterday at say, normal margin of 35%? As you may have guessed, the most profitable customer is the $195 customer. Or is it the customer who bought 10 times at $75 (some items were on sale, some not, but the average margin was 30%)?

To add more food for thought for those CFOs and VPs of major credit programs, if the $195 customer purchased on a special six-month no-interest, no-payment program and paid no interest and no payments for those six months, he was less profitable to your credit operation because it cost half of your gross margin to pay for the lost interest income. This type of factor can be built right into your database and used in the segmentation of your credit card customer base.

Contrary to the marketing direction and successes of just a few years ago, more is not more. If you do your homework and strive, through technology, to create great-grandpa's one-on-one customer relationships, you will find that in 1995 less is more. And in the decade of the 1990s, that strategy will identify the company managers who survive the highly competitive battle to gain market share with ever-shrinking margins.

IDEAL DATABASE MARKETING PROGRAM

☐ Collect important data on all cardholders.

☐ Carefully and professionally maintain the integrity of the data captured.

☐ Use some version of the recency, frequency, monetary value evaluation for your card base.

☐ Specifically target your customers to reduce marketing cost without decreasing sales.

☐ Take full advantage of the powerful information available through your database system to help other departments in the company such as merchandising, real estate, market research, and advertising.

☐ Learn or search out the best possible applications for your database.

DIRECT MAIL

Direct mail plays an important role in both the acquisition and activation of your credit card program. You will find more specific marketing approaches that utilize direct mail in Chapters 2 (prescreens), 8 (new resident), 9 (activation), and 11 (credit card reissue).

Direct mail is a highly sophisticated, complex, and disciplined tool in today's marketing environment. A few years ago, as a consumer, you expected most of the mail you received and therefore opened and read it.

In years past, as a business, you simply mailed whatever quantity your budget allowed, and the sales or responses came rolling in. Today, that approach will bankrupt you. Postage is higher, printing costs more, and response rates are down dramatically.

Therefore, before you mail anything, ask yourself this question: *Can your direct mail pass the three-second test?* The consumer who receives your direct mail package makes a decision to open it or throw it away in seconds. Look at your own mail today. Did you open all of it? Probably not (unless you are in the direct mail business). If you did open it, did you read all of the information enclosed? Probably not.

Direct mail and direct response advertising have become an art. Putting together a mail package requires a level of expertise just as complex as that needed for any other medium, such as radio, TV, or newspaper advertising.

Mail volume today exceeds 200 billion pieces a year. To ensure that your package stands out, this chapter provides some guidelines for planning and conducting a direct mail campaign.

TARGETING YOUR MARKET

Your first step should be to determine who will receive your direct mail package. Other chapters in this book give you pointers for specific programs. You should use absolutely *every* tool at your disposal to select the customer. Paramount to this is the use of database marketing and customer demographics. Literally every mailing can be segmented or segregated in one form or another. For example, if you are doing an activation mailing to your inactive accounts, there are many segments and categories of inactives: those who have not purchased in the last 90 days, or other segments of time; those who have never purchased; cardholders who respond only when promoted to, and so on.

If you are going to do a preapproved mailing, you will want to target your customer as much as possible. One way to do this is to do a demographic profile of your existing credit card customer base. This will tell you what your current cardholder looks like. Beyond that, you would want to look at the best-performing segments of your current cardholders and use this information to target your offer as precisely as possible. If you do not have the resources to completely analyze your card base then use general summary information from your new application processes. You can summarize the percentage of your current card base who are women, homeowners, have been at their residence or job for a certain period of time, and so on. These general summaries can help in the selection process when you get ready to rent names for a promotional mailing or to dissect your existing credit card base for a targeted mailing.

You can have a great offer on a great product at the right time of the year, but send it to the wrong customer and get dismal results.

CHOOSING YOUR MAILING LISTS

Be sure that your selected mailing list is up-to-date, accurate, and deliverable. You may be thinking, of course my own credit card list is up-to-date. Is it? Approximately 30% of Americans move every year. That is staggering.

If you are mailing to inactive accounts or to a compiled or rented list and have not run your list through an NCOA (National Change of Address), address correction requested, or other similar process, it is probably in poor shape. Remember too, that in today's postal environment of carrier routing, zip plus four, bulk rate, delivery to the BMC or SCF, your mail will no longer get to the desired person unless it is absolutely accurate. In some instances, even with what seems to be a complete name and address, some small amount of information may be incomplete. For example, the street address may read 123 Morningside, which looks just fine. However, the address is actually Morningside Ct., and it may or may not be properly delivered. Highly technical computer programs are available that can identify the insufficient addresses and correct them, or you may even want to eliminate them.

The postal service is very different from the mail delivery I grew up with. Sometimes, my grandmother would get a piece of mail with no street address, because, every postman knew everybody, and we didn't move nearly as much as people do now.

Most companies feel that the "or current occupant" option takes care of the undelivered problem. Only if you don't care who receives your offer. If you spent thousands of dollars to find a particular prospect who is highly likely to respond to your offer . . . and the person moved, did the "or current occupant" really do you any good?

DESIGNING YOUR DIRECT MAIL PACKAGE

Three seconds! That's all you have. You may have a great offer and send it to the ideal customer, but if the prospect doesn't even open it . . . well! Everything from the envelope to the material inside is so critical today that you should seek out the best vendor/partner experts available to help you. Your direct mail package must invoke a successful direct response while at the same time reflecting the corporate strategies and the image of your business.

Above all, *keep it simple.*

Imagine that you are writing your own resume. You start with the really powerful, important information to get across the enormous amount of talent, experience, and potential you can offer some prospective employer. Before you know it, you have written seven or eight pages and even then you think you left out a lot. Realistically, you accept that no prospective employer will sift through pages and pages of your vast experience no matter how good you are and you reduce this most important letter (your resume) to not more than two pages, perhaps even one.

It is much like that with your direct mail efforts. You start out with a great offer. Then you embellish it, add information about the services your business offers, locations, history of your company, details of the offer, and so on. There are ways to be effective without losing your customer in the process.

Exhibits 17-1 and 17-2 (see pp. 150–151) show two fictitious letters for you to review. Do you see a noticeable difference in their appeal?

The purpose of these two examples is to emphasize the value of the three-second rule. Version II quickly and clearly lets the customer know what the offer is. Notice how it passes the three-second test. I'm not a professional copy writer; that's why you have vendor/partners to help you. However, it is interesting to notice that both direct mail letters provide exactly the same information.

There are tons of techniques out there to help you drive home your message; here are just a few:

- Lift notes that usually say, "If you are not planning to respond, please read this."
- Response devices (e.g., place the enclosed gold seal on the order form).
- Rub-off cards with dots that are scratched off to reveal a discount.
- Personalization. Just look at your Publishers Clearing House mail package.
- Teasers on the outside of the envelope.
- Return addresses or no return addresses on the envelope.
- Postage meter imprint or live stamp?
- First-class postage or bulk-rate postage?

Exhibit 17-1
Version 1: Letter soliciting credit card accounts.

A & S Companies
5424 Henderson Rd., Hamptonville, NC 27020
1-800-472-3927

June 1, 1994

Bill Grady
5424 Henderson Rd.
Hamptonville, NC 27020

Dear Mr. Grady,
    We at A & S Companies are very proud of our 100 years of service to your community. We have even more to offer you today with our wide assortment and great prices. A special 10% off our everyday low prices, for you, our valued credit card customer, will save you even more.
    Be sure to come in and take advantage of our special Founder's Day event by this Saturday.
    We look forward to serving you in the near future.

Very truly yours,

Anthony Grady
President & CEO

Exhibit 17-2
Version 2: Letter soliciting credit card accounts.

A & S Companies
5424 Henderson Rd., Hamptonville, NC 27020
1-800-472-3927

10% OFF
Your Next Purchase

June 1, 1994

Bill Grady
5424 Henderson Rd.
Hamptonville, NC 27020

Dear Mr. Grady,

Save an extra 10% off your very next A & S Companies credit card purchase at A & S Company. We are very proud of our 100 years of service to your community and want to show our appreciation with this special 10% savings.

We have more to offer than ever—a wider assortment and our everyday low prices. Be sure to come in by this Saturday and bring this letter.

We look forward to serving you in the near future.

Very truly yours,

Anthony Grady
President & CEO

P.S. Don't miss this opportunity to save 10%.

- Urgent requests (e.g., Act fast . . . offer good 3 days only).
- Die cut, ink jet, cheshire, or gum label for the envelope.
- Color enhancement—One color, two color, three color, four color?
- Message on the back of envelope.
- Signed or unsigned? By whom?
- Coated or uncoated paper?
- Expensive look or discount look?
- Live stamp on the business reply envelope.
- Endorsements.

And many more. Your type of business, targeted audience, and budget will determine which techniques work best for you. Above all, test . . . test . . . test.

The most successful companies using direct mail are always testing.

As my friend Jack Kelly (VP of Sears Catalog, retired) has told me many times, "When you find something that works, use it until it stops working." All too often, companies try something and when it works, they say, "Well, that was great, now let's go find another winner," never again running the program that worked so beautifully.

In study after study, the Direct Marketing Association has determined that consumers nearly always look at a mail piece in this order:

1. The letterhead.
2. The greeting.
3. The signature.
4. The P.S.

At this point, if you are lucky, they will read the letter and check out the rest of the package. If you are really lucky, they will respond.

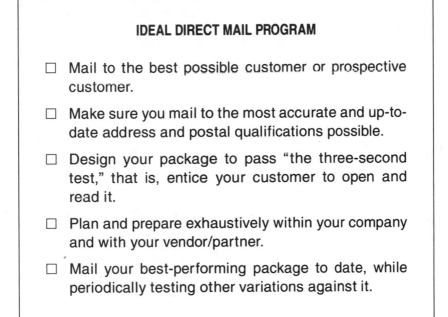

IDEAL DIRECT MAIL PROGRAM

☐ Mail to the best possible customer or prospective customer.

☐ Make sure you mail to the most accurate and up-to-date address and postal qualifications possible.

☐ Design your package to pass "the three-second test," that is, entice your customer to open and read it.

☐ Plan and prepare exhaustively within your company and with your vendor/partner.

☐ Mail your best-performing package to date, while periodically testing other variations against it.

TELEMARKETING

Telemarketing is another method of acquiring or activating credit card accounts. Usually, telemarketing of credit cards is used for prescreen or preapproved solicitations as well as for other purposes such as follow-up to store promotions. Some companies may use telemarketing only for their prescreen programs.

The most common prescreen use of telemarketing is as a follow-up to a direct mail program. At an appropriate time, when your mail responses have topped off and are winding down, you would de-dupe the mail responses to your prescreen and use a telemarketing vendor/partner to call the nonresponders and ask if they would like your company's credit card account.

I strongly recommend that you use only experienced, established telemarketing vendor/partners for this program. If used correctly by a quality vendor/partner, telemarketing can be an excellent marketing tool, while inferior telemarketing, like any other mishandled promotion, can be a serious problem.

In doing a telemarketing program, the vendor/partner you use will write a script (with your input) based on the objectives of your program. This is where you can avoid complaints about those high-pressure tactics so often associated with telemarketing. Pay close attention to the way you bridge from the objections consumers may express to the next level of information in helping them decide to accept your credit card. In the final analysis, your telemarketing program will only be a superficial success if you manage to open the targeted number of new accounts but alienate hundreds of current or potential customers or if you add thousands of new cardholders who really do not want your company's credit card.

Several techniques can help you avoid these problems, assuming you have paid meticulous attention to your telemarketing script. One of the most common procedures is to have a supervisor at the telemarketing vendor/partner re-call customers to verify the positive responses of respondents who replied affirmatively during the initial phone call.

Another technique is to have dial-in access or a special dedicated telephone for monitoring some of the telemarketing calls from time to time. Most reputable telemarketing companies regularly monitor calls anyway; however, it helps if they know you are interested enough to check in from time to time yourself.

SCHEDULING THE TELEMARKETING PROGRAM

Scheduling between the cutoff of your direct mail program, the de-duping of the mail responders, and the projected completion dates of your program is critical. These processes should be planned for and scheduled when you plan your entire prescreen program (see Chapter 2). This scheduling is extremely important if you are to maximize your overall results or if you are trying to add these new cardholders in time for a major promotion or your peak selling season.

The telemarketing vendor/partner will then prepare for your program by training the telemarketing staff, reserving the number of phones needed, and scheduling the times of the calls. Projecting the acceptance rate (number of people who accept your credit card) will enable the vendor to anticipate your targeted completion date.

Always be sure to keep your company's employees aware of your direct mail and telemarketing programs in case any customers call them to verify the legitimacy of the call they received or to ask questions about your offer. Your stores will almost certainly receive a few calls and personnel should be knowledgeable enough to support your efforts, not confuse or hinder them. Likewise, be sure your customer service and operations management at your credit card center are familiar with your program so they can field any call that may come in from either customers or store personnel.

MAXIMIZING THE RESULTS OF YOUR TELEMARKETING PROGRAM

The acceptance rate will vary greatly depending on the consumer offer you made and the reputation or appeal of your company. The number of acceptances by telemarketing will always be higher than your direct mail response; however, in many cases your activation of these accounts may be lower.

Here are a few suggestions to maximize your results:

- Use telemarketing as a follow-up to a direct mail program.
- Be sure your vendor/partner monitors a percentage of the calls made by the telemarketing representatives to verify compliance with your script and instructions.

- Re-call a percentage of those consumers accepting your credit card to verify their acceptance by the telemarketing vendor/partner you use.
- Calculate your per account cost or contract for a per acceptance cost unless you have an unlimited budget.
- Avoid using telemarketing vendor/partners who pay their telemarketing employee representatives based on the number of acceptances. This makes the representative aggressive and adds cardholders who will be very hard to activate. Ask them about this.
- Use a list of known shopping customers who are not cardholders first. If you do not have such a list, then use of a profile of your current customer base to rent similar customer names.
- If you have neither a current list of customers nor a profile of your current customers, use general demographic information such as income and homeownership to help better target the potential new cardholders.

MANAGING THE NUMBER OF NEW ACCOUNTS

To assist in estimating the number of accounts you can open or should open with telemarketing, let's look at a few guidelines and an example. My own personal rule of thumb is not to add more telemarketing accounts from my prescreen program than I acquired from my direct mail responses. In fact, I prefer to manage to a specific goal.

Let's say you mail 100,000 prescreen letters with a goal to get 10,000 accounts (10% response). If your mail response is 6% or 6,000 accounts, you would then want 4,000 telemarketing accounts. Since telemarketing responders generally tend to be less active than mail responders, this will help keep your activation rates for your prescreen in balance.

Some companies feel differently and call everyone to get every single account possible. Unfortunately, this approach may add an excessive number of accounts that may never activate but that gross up the future cost of all your activation promotions and mailings because they are in the card base.

Another key factor is the proximity of the consumer to your bank or retail location. Even though you may pull some business from many miles away, your likelihood of having customers shop or bank with you diminishes quickly after a distance of about 5 miles (depending on the type of retail business you have). A general guideline is that metropolitan or urban locations usually have a smaller primary trading area than more rural or mid-sized markets.

CONTROLLING TELEMARKETING COSTS

You may find that the cost estimates you receive from various telemarketing vendor/partners will be quite different. Most telemarketing vendor/partners will probably quote you a per hour rate. Some will quote you a per account rate, and still others will quote you on a per contact basis. If the telemarketing vendor/partner has no experience with your bank or retail operation or with a very similar operation, they will almost certainly quote you a per hour rate because the success of each telemarketing contact will depend on many factors such as the following ones:

- The reputation of your bank or retail business.
- The market awareness of your business.
- The strength of your offer (e.g., low APR, free gift, no annual fee).
- The location of your place of business.

Since the only thing the telemarketing vendor/partner can control is the professionalism and training of their employees, they may be unsure about the positive response rate you may have. Therefore, if they priced you per acceptance (customers who said yes to your phone offer), and you had a very low acceptance rate, they would not make a profit on your program. However, if you pay an hourly rate and you have a poor acceptance, then your costs per account will be very high. For that reason, whenever possible, you probably will want to try to control your costs by negotiating a per acceptance rate.

TRACKING RESULTS: RESPONSE RATES

Response rates can vary widely, but here are some general ranges that should help you estimate your potential results and costs. Telemarketing solicitations will almost always run at least 3 times, normally 5 or 6 times, and sometimes 10 to 12 times the response rate you attain with direct mail prescreens. For example, if you normally get about a 5% response to a direct mail prescreen program, you could expect to get from 15% to 60% acceptance from your telemarketing program. As a broad rule of thumb, of the contacts made, you will usually get about a 30% acceptance based on the variables mentioned earlier. A percentage of your targeted audience will not be home at the time of the call or the primary person called will not be home, and that factor alone will reduce the opportunity for a greater response.

SUMMARY

Telemarketing should be a solid part of your direct mail campaign if used properly. After all, you have already incurred the cost to obtain the consumer name list, paid the credit bureau to pass your credit criteria, invested in premiums or other offers all aimed at a fast increase in your credit card account base. But, also keep in mind that these telemarketing accounts may be less active, so do all you can to balance the number of telemarketing accounts with your direct mail accounts to keep the activation rates in line.

IDEAL TELEMARKETING PROGRAM

☐ Target your telemarketing efforts to your best customers first (best profile customer for T&E cards).

☐ Call potential customers who are within five miles of your branch, retail location, or convenience store location (best profile for T&E).

☐ Use your telemarketing campaign as a follow-up to your prescreen direct mail program.

☐ Usually keep the number of telemarketing accounts opened equal to or less than the number of direct mail responders received.

☐ Carefully choose a reliable telemarketing vendor/ partner who is familiar and experienced with the credit industry.

ADVERTISING

Advertising is a grossly underutilized area of credit card marketing. This is unfortunate since credit card marketing and promotional efforts have a significant positive impact on overall sales. In light of this, the most successful businesses generally adopt a comprehensive approach to advertising that carefully highlights the credit program's special role in growing sales.

In advertising, assumptions can be dangerous. I always try to remember the guidance that Bob Strickland, Chairman of the Board of Lowe's Companies, gave me when he said, "We sometimes think that consumers know certain things that are second nature to us; little things like where your store is located, what you sell, when you are open, and whether you have a credit card program or not."

The wisdom of Bob's words is continuously reinforced when I see newspaper advertisements that fail to disclose store locations. Sure, everybody knows where XYZ company is, . . . or do they? Nearly 30% of a city's population moves each year, which means there will always be new customers who may not know about your company.

Have you ever received a prescreen or preapproved offer for a credit card in the mail from XYZ company, but you had no idea what the firm sells or where it is located?

IMPACT OF ADVERTISING ON CREDIT CARD PROGRAMS

Credit and advertising interact in powerful ways, as illustrated by the case of a retailer who had a "closed door" sale, open only to holders of the store's private label credit card. Nearly half the sales during the promotion were paid for by cash or other payment type besides the private label card. The bond or franchise that exists between the cardholders and the retailer helped motivate the customers' response to the promotion, even though many of them chose a different payment type.

In another example, a large prescreen mailing was made just prior to the grand opening of a new store. While 10% of the consumers who received the prescreen package responded by mail, many other consumers who did not respond still come to the grand opening. Even though these customers did not accept the credit card, the prescreen made them aware of the event and stimulated interest and sales.

It is in your best interest to share the sales and results of your credit card program with your advertising, marketing, and executive management. Through regular communication, you can show your advertising department that your credit card program is an important product and service, very much like the merchandise or other services that you sell. After all, the credit card vehicle often generates over half your company's business. Be forewarned that your merchandising department may not easily give up space for their products, but the best-run and most successful companies are always careful to highlight their credit card and the special promotions available with it.

PRINT MEDIA

These include ROP newspaper coverage, catalogs, magazines, and flyers or tabs. Some companies do a great job, while some do practically nothing at all. The absence of advertising support for your credit program is a sad commentary for a vehicle that, in many instances, represents 20% to 60% of a company's total business.

It's not uncommon to find advertising departments whose philosophy is that it is sufficient to show a minuscule replica of the credit cards the company accepts, often buried in the ad. The advertising term for this small block of logos is called a "slug," an appropriate term if this is all the exposure you give to your credit card program. In reality, this block of logos can be a valuable marketing tool that should always be included on any printed advertisement as part of the standard layout. Unfortunately, some companies devote more space to explaining their layaway or rain-check programs than their credit card. Think about it.

You can enhance the standard slug by adding useful information that addresses customer needs such as "Instant Credit Available" or "90 Days Interest Free." The idea is to turn the slug into a proactive, permanent marketing tool. An example of a slug is shown in Exhibit 19-1.

Next you may want occasional feature or subfeature space in the print ad for a specific credit card event, for example, "6 Months Interest Free" or "Only 9.4% APR." An example of

Exhibit 19-1
Typical newspaper ad.

XYZ Company
MEMORIAL DAY SALE

LARGE ASSORTMENT OF BICYCLES

SAVE ON ALL TV'S, STEREOS, AND CAMCORDERS

XYZ Company
123 Main St.
Anytown, USA

Exhibit 19-2
Typical Newspaper ad with credit card promotion.

how to feature a credit card event in an ROP advertisement is shown in Exhibit 19-2.

All advertisements should inform your customers or prospective customers about your credit card program and any special credit card events. Some companies will occasionally include a credit card application or toll-free number in their catalogs or flyers.

Take a look at your print advertising, and lobby for your fair share exposure. Schedule your special programs around other marketing promotions and during peak selling seasons. You can always find room to include your credit card program if you will make the effort.

ELECTRONIC MEDIA

These include television, radio, and interactive kiosk. While time in these mediums can be costly, a 20- to 60-second commercial spot can lend itself nicely to promoting your credit card. Freestanding kiosks are now gaining in popularity and usage. This entire kiosk revolution did not take hold until the banks were able to gain customer acceptance of the ATM (Automatic Teller Machine) networks.

There are any number of ways to "work your credit card in" to these advertising media. Radio or TV spots, much like print media, can feature your credit card or simply tag it into the product or services offered. For example, a company selling a particular product or service may show the customer paying with the company's own credit card.

Appliance and furniture retailers will often center their commercial spots around "6 Months Interest Free" or "Payments as Low as $15.00 per Month." For big ticket, durable goods, credit cards are a more important advertising and marketing focus. Most of the emphasis with these retailers will be no-interest or no-payment promotions. Sales results are tied directly to the length of time of the interest-free or deferred payment period. For example, no payments and no interest for 90 days will give you a reasonable sales lift, but the same offer for 6 months or even for 12 months will increase sales dramatically. It will increase costs dramatically too, but you can easily weigh the value of the gross margin generated versus the lost interest income. The primary medium of choice for these retailers is print, with some television.

Bankcards often feature their new low APR or no annual fee Visa or MasterCard. In today's security-minded environment, Citibank has even found value in advertising a picture ID on their Visa. Television and magazines are the primary media of choice for banks.

T&E companies and affinity cards typically showcase frequent flier programs, extended warranties, or lost or stolen card replacement services. All media apply to this group with heavy magazine concentration followed closely by television.

Some retail chains will show an actor promoting a particular product in their television commercials the actor pays for the product with the store's credit card. Others will show their credit card at the end of the television spot. These "trailers," as they are called in television production, can be effective ways to show the credit cards you accept. With the explosion of TV home shopping networks and programs, credit cards have become an indispensable means of payment.

On radio, you can talk about the features or benefits that sets your credit card apart from other cards. As in your print media, you can work copy into your radio script such as ". . . and you can charge it on your XYZ credit card." Or mention that instant credit is available when you visit the store.

You really shouldn't expect (nor would you want) your credit card program to dominate your company's advertising. However, your credit card program can't help you if it's obscured, hidden, or not included at all.

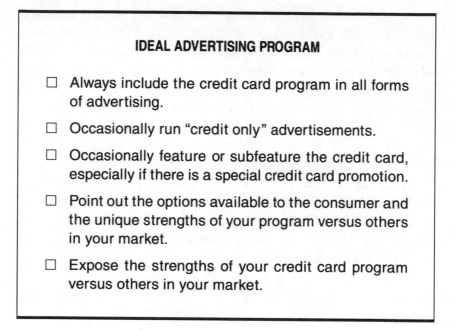

IDEAL ADVERTISING PROGRAM

☐ Always include the credit card program in all forms of advertising.

☐ Occasionally run "credit only" advertisements.

☐ Occasionally feature or subfeature the credit card, especially if there is a special credit card promotion.

☐ Point out the options available to the consumer and the unique strengths of your program versus others in your market.

☐ Expose the strengths of your credit card program versus others in your market.

INTEREST-FREE, DEFERRED PAYMENT, AND SKIP PAYMENT PROMOTIONS

Interest-free, deferred payment, and skip payment promotions have been around for years. Recently, particularly in the retail sector, the interest-free and deferred payment promotions have become much more prevalent. These programs are sometimes referred to as credit-based promotions.

You may recall a television commercial or newspaper advertisement that says, "Buy today on our credit card program and pay no interest for 90 days." Usually, you will see more promotions of this type at big ticket retailers, such as appliance dealers and furniture stores, where such offers have almost become permanent fixtures.

There are any number of variations of this type of promotion such as:

1. No interest and no payment for 90 days.
2. No interest and no payment for 6 months.

171

3. Buy today and pay no interest until next year (payments required).

4. No interest for 12 months.

5. Purchase over $200 on your credit card today and make no payments until next year.

The value of this type of promotion is that it allows consumers to purchase something they want or need now without paying any interest or in some cases without having to make any payments until a later date. For the retailer, this type of promotion can draw customers away from competitors or help kick-start preseason sales. For example, buy your lawn tractor in March and make no payments until July. You buy the mower early in the season and then start your payments when you are actually using it the most.

In most industries, interest-free promotions tend to attract more affluent customers because they have the money to pay off their purchase within the interest-free period and therefore are basically using the float of your company's money to their advantage.

The cost to run interest-free or deferred payment programs varies greatly. The two single biggest factors in determining the cost are the length of time involved and how many of your customers actually pay the balance in full within the interest-free period. The cost is higher in these instances because of the lost finance charge revenues and the retailer's cost of funds during the free period.

PLANNING THE PROMOTION

Many retailers today use the interest-free and no-payment plans to boost their average sales figures. You do this by setting a targeted purchase amount. For example, if your average purchase is $85, you would advertise no interest or no payments on purchases of $200 or more for a specified period of time. You will usually use this type of offer during a particular holiday or seasonal event such as Mother's Day or Fourth of July promotions. If you have the appetite to cover the lost finance income revenues, you could run Christmas in July with purchases made in July exempt from payments or interest until the next year (six months).

Some retailers, primarily appliance and electronics chains, will target specific high-end merchandise. You could promote no interest or no payments on selected rooms of furniture or specific electronic purchases. A few manufacturers even have their own private label branded credit cards, which usually offer these no-interest and no-payment options for their brand of merchandise only. These credit promotions can be very powerful, but they can also be very costly to the retailer or manufacturer. It all depends on the number of customers who pay off within the specified time and therefore pay no finance charges.

Another version of these types of programs, used by banks and retailers alike, is a skip payment program. Credit card customers are advised through billing statement messages or inserts that they can skip a particular payment if they choose to. This type of promotion does not stimulate sales as much, but rather helps increase your interest income. Another version shows customers that they are prepaid for that month's payment. Usually, the finance charges continue to accrue. A majority of all credit card banks and retailers will offer this option during the Christmas season.

The interest-free, deferred payment, and skip payment programs are especially effective as disaster relief tools. In natural disasters such as hurricanes or floods, credit card issuers can help the victims by offering skip payment plans, interest-free options, or deferred payment programs.

Every credit card issuer should have a disaster plan ready at all times. Some options that may be included besides the skip payment or interest-free plans include automatic credit limit increases. For example, when the Midwest was devastated by flooding, cardholders were allowed to cycle their payments for several months and were offered assistance in other ways. Dropping your APR or offering an interest-free period and an immediate across-the-board credit limit increase after a disaster will demonstrate your company's compassion and community spirit as well as attract a significant amount of business.

For the credit-based promotions to be most effective, you should plan them into your annual promotional calendar. For some companies, quarterly promotions are in order. Others tend to run these types of promotions almost year-round. In any event, credit-based promotions have a place in almost every company's credit marketing plan.

IDEAL CREDIT-BASED PROMOTION

☐ Schedule it preseason to take sales out of the market just before the peak selling season.

☐ Do not promote longer than six months in advance, to keep your cost within an acceptable range.

☐ Offer both no-payment and no-interest plans to appeal to the widest customer base. (However, interest would accrue and revert to the day of purchase if not paid in full.)

☐ Advertise to be competitive within your market.

CREDIT CARD MARKETING PLAN

Right now, some of you who are reading this book manage the marketing and promotional efforts for a credit card program but do not have a credit marketing plan. You probably have a budget and some specific promotional goals but not a marketing plan. Likewise, some of us have a credit marketing plan, but it is incomplete or has not changed for years.

To illustrate the power and necessity of an accurate, annual, detailed marketing plan, consider the following case study.

Let's say your company is located in Cincinnati, Ohio, and headquarters announces a big business and pleasure meeting has been scheduled. There are a few things you need to know. Where is the meeting? What are the dates of the meeting? These could be considered goals or objectives. In much the same way, you would need to know the goal or objective of your credit card program for next year. "All you can get" is not a goal.

177

Your meeting is in Orlando, Florida, 30 days from today. Do you now jump in your car, rush to the nearest airport, get on the next plane out (wherever that plane may be going), and travel around the United States until you end up in Orlando, Florida (if you ever do)? You could pass through Orlando, you know, by sheer luck. Drive around or fly around enough and you could coincidentally end up in Orlando. Of course, it may be 10 years from now and your meeting would have long since concluded, but it is possible. Don't laugh. I have reviewed some credit marketing programs that succeeded by sheer luck alone . . . but not very many.

Some of you may think I am being ridiculous. Well, I have consulted and worked with some pretty large corporations whose credit card managers tell me their goal is to get all the credit card accounts they can. They then wistfully comment that they wanted to do $x sales volume on those accounts this year. However, they missed their goal and just aren't too sure why. While they may have a clear objective for a particular promotional program, such as a prescreen, there is no cohesive plan showing what part that prescreen plays in reaching their nebulous goal of "all we can get."

Back to our meeting in Orlando. Shouldn't you think about travel options (car, plane, train, etc.)? What about pulling out your road map to check the best routes (programs) to get you there? If you fly, will you rent a car at the airport in Orlando so you can get to the meeting? This whole exercise underscores the absolute necessity of having a strong, credible, marketing plan for your credit card program.

HOW TO DEVELOP A SOLID MARKETING PLAN

First you must determine your goal or receive your goal from your upper management. It doesn't matter what form the goal takes. I will show you how to turn the goal into a sound marketing plan. Another one of my rules of thumb is that you should never have an acquisition marketing plan that does not include activation, nor should you have an activation marketing plan that excludes acquisition. You are constantly running like an engine, alternating between activation and acquisition. The way you direct your marketing efforts is driven by your goal and the maturity of your credit card program. For example, if you are just starting a brand-new credit card program for your business you may spend 80% of your available budget on acquisition and 20% on activation. With a mature credit card program, you are more likely to spend 80% of your available marketing budget on activation and 20% on acquisition. Now back to how you turn your goals into a sound marketing plan.

Your goal may be any one of the following:

- Bring in $100,000,000 in credit card sales this year.
- Open 200,000 new accounts this year.
- Invest your $300,000 budget to maximize ROI.
- Increase credit penetration from 30% to 35%.
- Make a gross margin contribution of $250,000.

All these targets can and should be broken down into the number of accounts needed or activation results needed, or both, to achieve your goal.

For example, consider the first goal listed: to bring in $100,000,000 in credit card sales this year. Your existing credit card base produced $75,000,000 in sales last year so you must get at least another $25,000,000 in new sales. Here's the formula to use:

You need to know your average annual purchases from your existing card base per cardholder and the average approval and acquisition rates (ideally by source of acquisition). To keep our example simple, we will use annual sales of $1,000, an approval rate of 50%, and an activation rate of 50%.

Sales goal of $25,000,000 divided by $1,000 average annual sales equals 25,000 new active accounts needed, divided by 50% activation equals 50,000 total accounts needed, divided by 50% approval rate equals 100,000 applications needed.

You also know that you need these accounts between January 1 and December 31. So we now know where we are going and when we need to get there. Next, we must determine how we are going to get there. Now the planning begins.

You can use prescreens, hostess programs, take-one programs, new resident programs, telemarketing, employee contests, activation programs, and so on—some or all of the above.

A multifaceted, balanced approach for your business is always preferable. Let's face it—not everyone responds to a prescreen program. In fact, only a small percentage do. However, the person who throws your mail piece away may respond by telemarketing. People who will not respond by mail or phone may apply because a professional hostess offers them a free gift. Those who do not want a free gift and will not respond by mail or phone may apply through an employee of your company, who in turn is motivated by an employee incentive. And, none of the above may appeal to some people, who may prefer to pick up a take-one application and apply.

In addition, you must allow for the activation rates, approval rates, and sales levels for each of the individual types of promotions or marketing approaches.

DEVELOPING YOUR MARKETING PLAN

In developing a plan to reach your goal ($100,000,000 in credit card sales this year), look at your history and calculate your requirements for each marketing option.

Take-One Applications.   If you have been averaging 5,000 mail-in (take-one) applications per month this past year, you can expect to receive the same next year, unless you decide to expand or enhance the take-one program. So let's analyze the mail-in applications:

5,000 take-one applications per month × 12 months = 60,000 annually

If approval rate for take-ones is 50%,

60,000 × 50% = 30,000 approved new accounts

If activation rate for take-ones is 50%,

30,000 new accounts × 50% = 15,000 new active accounts

If average sales per account annually is $1,000,

15,000 new active accounts × $1,000 = $15,000,000 in new credit card sales

Cost. We have calculated our printing cost and business reply postage cost will be $30,000.

We now know that we need another 10,000 active accounts from other sources and another $10,000,000 in sales volume.

Do a Prescreen Program.   We don't have an unlimited budget, so we will mail to about 200,000 names, as we did last year. If we have about 600,000 customer names available from our in-house mailing list or database, we will use those. Since the pass rate at the credit bureau tends to be approximately one-third, we can expect to have the 200,000 names we want to mail. From last year's prescreen program, we know we had a 7% response, so we can use that as our guideline for next year's program:

$$200{,}000 \times 7\% \text{ mail response} = 14{,}000 \text{ accounts}$$

To maximize our prescreen investment, we want to get a total of 10% or 20,000 accounts. So let's telemarket to get another 6,000 accounts. The activation rate is slightly lower for the telemarketing accounts so we will apply that experience to our pro forma.

$$14{,}000 \text{ mail responses @ } 50\% \text{ activation} = 7{,}000$$

$$6{,}000 \text{ telemarketing responses @ } 40\% \text{ activation} = 2{,}400$$

This gives us a total of 9,400 active accounts @ $1,000 in annual sales each for a total of $9,400,000 in sales.

Cost. We have received quotes from our direct mail and telemarketing vendor/partners and estimate our cost to be approximately $120,000.

Look at an Employee Contest.   It will give you active accounts, and it also has the residual effect of training our employees.

Let's establish a goal of 100 credit card applications per store during a six-week period. If we have 100 stores, then our expected total applications would be 100 stores × 100 applications = 10,000 applications:

10,000 applications × 50% approval =
5,000 approved accounts

5,000 approved accounts × 50% activation rate =
2,500 total active accounts

2,500 active accounts × annual purchases of $1,000 =
$2,500,000 in sales next year

Cost. We anticipate paying about $3.00 per application, which means our cost for this program will be $30,000.

Continue the New Resident Program.   We have had a new resident program for the past few years. Relatively few people move within our markets monthly; we have been averaging about 5,000 per month:

5,000 new resident applications per month × 12 months =
60,000 applications

Note: We could prescreen these as well; however, for the sake of our example we will not.

60,000 applications × response rate of 15% =
9,000 new resident applications for our credit card

9,000 applications × 50% approval rate =
4,500 new accounts

4,500 new accounts × 50% activation rate =
2,250 active accounts

2,250 active accounts × $1,500 in average annual sales =
$3,375,000 in annual sales

Note: A new resident application tends to have higher annual purchases than the average of the card base.

Cost. This program has been included in the corporate advertising budget annually since we are only riding along with them. Our part of this cost is $20,000.

Plan a Hostess Program.   We know one new store will be opened next year so a hostess program could coincide with that grand opening.

One new store hostess program based on your previous grand opening experience usually produces 10,000 applications:

$$10{,}000 \text{ hostess applications} \times 50\% \text{ approval} =$$
$$5{,}000 \text{ new accounts}$$

$$5{,}000 \text{ new accounts} \times 60\% \text{ activation} =$$
$$3{,}000 \text{ active accounts}$$

Note: Hostess applications tend to be more active than the average of your card base.

$$3{,}000 \text{ active accounts} \times \$1{,}000 \text{ average annual sales} =$$
$$\$3{,}000{,}000 \text{ in sales}$$

Cost. This program is expensed to the new store grand opening expense and does not come directly from our credit card marketing budget.

Include an Activation Program.   We want to have an activation mailing to all our inactive accounts (no sales transaction with us within the last six months). By analyzing our credit card master file, we determine that 100,000 cardholders meet this criteria. From our past experience, we know that by offering these cardholders a 10% discount 15% will activate their account and make a purchase of approximately $100.

$$100,000 \text{ cardholders} \times 15\% =$$
$$15,000 \text{ cardholders activate}$$

$$15,000 \times \text{the average purchase of } \$100 =$$
$$\$1,500,000 \text{ in sales}$$

Cost. We solicit bids from our direct mail vendor/partners and know that this program will cost us $40,000.

ASSEMBLE ALL YOUR INFORMATION

You would perform an analysis like the preceding exercises for each type of promotion you might want to use during the next year, based on the amount of budget available but always keeping in mind your goal. If these programs exceed your available funding, you would have to trim or eliminate portions of one or more of your programs. Or, you may have to concentrate most of your funds in the one area where you get the absolute best returns and reduce your efforts elsewhere.

We have addressed the first goal of $100,000,000 in credit card sales for next year; however, perhaps the budget required to achieve the goal is more than your senior management planned to spend. This process enables you to know where you stand so you can either increase the budget or reduce the sales expectations now rather than waiting until the middle of next year to discover that things aren't working out as you had anticipated.

You can also easily adjust any of the programs you need. By using your road map, you can develop a promotional calendar or marketing planning calendar, and you can assign time frames and accountabilities for the proper execution to achieve your goals.

By putting the key activities on a marketing calendar and carefully watching the results of each program, you will immediately know if you are on target during the next year. For example, if your employee contest comes in 2,000 applications short, you know right then that you need to make these 2,000 applications up on some other program or adjust your total expected sales for the year downward to be in line with the shortfall. In other words, you are now managing your credit card program rather than having it manage (or surprise) you or your management.

DRAFT A WRITTEN PLAN

Each of these programs should be put into written form as part of a presentation. It should begin with an executive summary that reviews the total marketing plan and objectives in the detail needed to substantiate your projections. Also, senior management can then easily determine if your funding or objectives are in line with the company's strategic plan.

Appendix A illustrates the executive summary and analysis formulas. In addition, blank worksheets are provided to help you learn how to easily calculate the cost of a particular program versus the actual sales expected. These forms are somewhat simplified to conform with the space limitations of this book. You must undertake a great deal of analysis, research, and study of historical information before you can accurately project all the cost and sales numbers involved.

You should prepare a marketing or promotional calendar listing the important parts of your program to ensure proper execution and follow-through.

IDEAL CREDIT MARKETING PLAN

☐ Have a clear goal.

☐ Address the goal in a comprehensive fashion, yielding the best return on investment.

☐ Include both the cost and sales expected.

☐ Always be as accurate as possible.

☐ Coordinate with your company's overall marketing and advertising strategy.

☐ Include an executive summary, followed by detailed tactical objectives.

APPENDIX A

SAMPLE MARKETING PLAN

CREDIT MARKETING PLAN

FISCAL YEAR 19 _ _

EXECUTIVE SUMMARY

19 _ _   Goal is: $100,000,000.00 in credit card sales.

Budget allocated is: $500,000.00.

Our objective will be to achieve our sales goal utilizing a comprehensive credit marketing program that ensures the best results at the lowest cost possible. This achievement will maximize the ROI for our credit card program.

Our credit marketing plan for fiscal year 19 _ _   will cover:

• Take-One Applications	• Prescreen Programs	• New Resident Programs
• Employee Contest	• Hostess Programs	• Activation Programs
• Telemarketing	• Activation Programs	• Advertising Support
• In-Store Signing	• Training	• Instant Credit

EXECUTIVE SUMMARY
SALES and EXPENSES for 19 _ _

	TOTAL APPLICATIONS	TOTAL ACCOUNTS	COST	FULL YEAR SALES*
Take-One Applications and Store Signing Packages	60,000	30,000	supplies exp	$15,000,000
Employee Contest	10,000	5,000	$ 30,000	3,375,000
Hostess Program				
Prescreen Program	20,000	20,000	120,000	9,400,000
Spring Activation				
Fall Activation				
Interest-Free Promotion				
TOTAL				
Est. Sales/Existing Card Base				
GRAND TOTAL				
New Store Prescreen and Hostess Program				

* This is an example only; columns are not completely filled in.

TAKE-ONE APPLICATIONS

Pro Forma Sales Analysis

Based on the average number of applications processed per store
    (_____ stores)

EACH MONTH	TOTAL MONTHLY APPLICATIONS	TOTAL ANNUAL APPLICATIONS
_____	_____	_____

_____ total annual applications × 50% approval rate = _____ accounts

_____ accounts × 50% activation rate* = _____ active accounts

_____ active accounts × $_____ average annual purchase =
    $_____ annual sales

*Activation rates are based on a period of one year from date account opened.

EMPLOYEE CONTEST

Pro Forma Sales Analysis

Six weeks with a goal of _____ applications per store (_____) stores × (goal) = _____ applications

_____ applications × \$3.00 cost per application = \$_____

_____ applications × 50% approval rate = _____ accounts

_____ accounts × 50% activation rate = _____ active accounts

_____ active accounts × \$ _____ average annual purchases = \$_____

HOSTESS PROGRAMS

Pro Forma Sales Analysis

_____ new store grand openings × goal of _____ applications
per opening = _____

_____ hostess applications × 50% approval rate = _____ accounts

_____ approved accounts × 50% activation rate = _____ active accounts

_____ active accounts × $_____ average annual sales per account =
$_____

_____ applications @ $_____ cost per application = $_____ total cost

PRESCREEN—EXISTING STORES

Pro Forma Sales Analysis

_____ customer names @ 33% Credit Bureau Pass = _____ net names

_____ % mail response = _____ mail accounts

_____ telemarketing response = _____ telemarketing accounts
                                    Total number of prescreen accounts opened _____

_____ mail accounts × _____ % activation rate = _____ active mail accounts

_____ telemarketing accounts × _____ % activation rate =
_____ active telemarketing accounts
                        Total number of active prescreen accounts _____

_____ active accounts × $_____ average annual purchases =
$_____ annual sales

Cost: _____ mail packages @ $_____ each = $_____
      _____ telemarketing accounts @ $_____ each = $_____
                            Grand total prescreen cost = $_____

SPRING ACTIVATION PROGRAM

Pro Forma Sales Analysis

Targeted goal is _____ inactive accounts @ _____ response rate @ average purchase of $_____ = total sales of $_____.

Mailing cost: _____ mail packages @ $_____ each = $_____

Premium cost: _____ responses $\times$ $_____ cost per premium = $_____

APPENDIX B

VENDORS AND SUPPLIERS

ASSOCIATIONS

American Assoc. of Creditor Attys
2140 11th Ave. South, Suite 315
Birmingham, AL 35205
Phone: 205-939-0554

American Bankers Association
1120 Connecticut Ave. NW
Washington, DC 20036
Phone: 202-663-5000

Associated Credit Bureaus, Inc.
1790 Vermont Ave. NW, Suite 200
Washington, DC 20005-4905
Phone: 202-371-0910

Bank Administration Institute
2550 Golf Rd.
Rolling Meadows, IL 60008
Phone: 800-323-8552

Bank Marketing Association
309 W. Washington St.
Chicago, IL 60606
Phone: 312-782-1442

Bankcard Holders of America
560 Herndon Pkwy., Suite 120
Herndon, VA 22070
Phone: 703-481-1110

BankCard Services Assoc.
3101 Broadway, Suite 585
Kansas City, MO 64111
Phone: 800-695-5509

Bankers Institute
21 Tamal Vista Blvd.
Corte Madera, CA 94925
Phone: 415-924-1420

Consumer Bankers Assoc.
1000 Wilson Blvd., Suite 3012
Arlington, VA 22209
Phone: 703-276-1750

Credit Union National Assoc.
5710 Mineral Point Rd.
Madison, WI 53705
Phone: 608-231-4000

Direct Marketing Association
11 W. 42nd St.
New York, NY 10036
Phone: 212-719-5106

Electronic Data Interchange
  Assoc.
225 Reinekers Ln., Suite 550
Alexandria, VA 22314
Phone: 703-838-8042

Electronic Funds Transfer Assoc.
1421 Prince St., Suite 310
Alexandria, VA 22314
Phone: 703-549-9800

Independent Bankers Assoc.
1525 Wilson Blvd., Suite 540
Arlington, VA 22209
Phone: 703-841-5102

International Card Manuf. Assoc.
14 Washington Rd., Building 5
Princeton Junction, NJ 08550
Phone: 609-799-4900

International Consumer Credit
  Assoc.
243 N. Lindbergh Blvd.
St. Louis, MO 63141
Phone: 314-991-3030

MasterCard International
888 7th Ave.
New York, NY 10106
Phone: 212-649-4600

Nat. Automated Clearing House
  Assoc.
607 Herndon Pkwy., Suite 200
Herndon, VA 22070
Phone: 703-742-9190

Nat. Organization of Clearing
  Houses
607 Herndon Pkwy., Suite 200
Herndon, VA 22070
Phone: 703-742-9190

National Retail Federation—CMD
100 W. 31st St.
New York, NY 10001-3401
Phone: 212-563-5113

Shared Network Executives Assn.
600 Travis St., Suite 942
Houston, TX 77002
Phone: 713-223-1400

U.S. League of Savings Inst.
111 E. Wacker Dr.
Chicago, IL 60601
Phone: 312-938-2565

Visa USA
P.O. Box 8999
San Francisco, CA 94128-8999
Phone: 415-570-3200

ATM KIOSKS AND SURROUNDS

Acme Wiley Corp.
2480 Greenleaf Ave.
Elk Grove Village, IL 60007
Phone: 708-364-2250

Carter-Miot Engineering Co.
1829 Shop Rd.
Columbia, SC 29201
Phone: 803-771-4005

Companion Systems, Inc.
645 W. 200 North
North Salt Lake, UT 84054
Phone: 801-298-8082

E. F. Couvrette Co., Inc.
11478 Woodside Ave.
Santee, CA 92071
Phone: 619-448-1114

Cutler Industries, Inc.
Rt. 13, Box 707
Bristol, PA 19007
Phone: 800-548-5231

Dallman Industrial Corp.
933 N. Illinois St.
Indianapolis, IN 46204
Phone: 317-634-7774

Doane & Williams
307 Meadow St.
Chicopee, MA 01013
Phone: 800-242-1142

Heflin Building Systems, Inc.
1201 W. Arbrook Blvd., Suite 109A
Arlington, TX 76015
Phone: 817-467-2933

InterBold
P.O. Box 3091
North Canton, OH 44720
Phone: 216-497-5099

Lauretano Sign Corp.
700 Emmett St.
Bristol, CT 06010
Phone: 203-582-0233

Manufactured Buildings, Inc.
12690 60th St. North
Clearwater, FL 34620
Phone: 813-536-9437

Siemens Nixdorf Inf. Systems
200 Wheeler Rd.
Burlington, MA 01803
Phone: 617-273-0480

Simpson Sign Co.
1000 Washington Ave.
Croydon, PA 19021
Phone: 215-788-5515

ATM TERMINAL MFG.

ATM Exchange
5660 Wooster Rd.
Cincinnati, OH 45227
Phone: 513-272-1081 (Used)

Concord Computing Corp.
1713 Carmen Dr.
Elk Grove Village, IL 60007
Phone: 708-593-2044

EFMARK
777 Oakmont Ln., Suite 200
Westmont, IL 60559
Phone: 513-272-1081 (Used)

Fujitsu Systems of America, Inc.
12670 High Bluff Dr.
San Diego, CA 92130
Phone: 619-481-4004

InterBold
P.O. Box 3091
North Canton, OH 44720
Phone: 216-497-5099

NCR Corporation
1700 S. Patterson Blvd.
Dayton, OH 45479
Phone: 513-445-5000

Neuron Electronics, Inc.
3914 Del Ano Blvd.
Torrance, CA 90503
Phone: 213-793-1300

Omron Systems of America, Inc.
1300 Basswood Rd.
Schaumburg, IL 60173
Phone: 708-843-0515

The Oliver Allen Corp.
30 El Portal
Sausalito, CA 94965
Phone: 415-332-6262 (Used)

AUTO DIALING EQUIPMENT

Arkansas Systems, Inc.
8901 Kanis Rd.
Little Rock, AR 72205
Phone: 501-227-8471

Catmark, Inc.
967 E. Swedeford Rd., Suite 501
Exton, PA 19341
Phone: 215-651-0377

Davox Corp.
3 Federal St.
Billerica, MA 01821
Phone: 508-667-4455

Digital Systems Int., Inc.
7659 178th Place NE
Redmond, WA 98073-0908
Phone: 206-881-7544

Electronic Information Sys., Inc.
1351 Washington Blvd.
Stamford, CT 06902
Phone: 203-351-4800

Information Access Technology,
    Inc.
1100 E. 6600 South, Suite 300
Salt Lake City, UT 84121
Phone: 801-265-8800

International Telesystems
600 Herndon Pkwy.
Herndon, VA 22070
Phone: 800-955-7744

Melita Electronic Labs
6630 Bay Circle
Norcross, GA 30071
Phone: 404-446-7800

TeleSystems Marketing, Inc.
17440 N. Dallas Pkwy., Suite 120
Dallas, TX 75287
Phone: 214-248-3686

CARD ENHANCEMENT COS.

Allstate Life Insurance Co.
1415 Lake-Cook Rd.
Deerfield, IL 60015
Phone: 703-317-6251

Amerenhance
9779 M Street
Omaha, NE 68127
Phone: 402-592-4111

American Bankers Ins. Group
11222 Quail Roost Dr.
Miami, FL 33157-6596
Phone: 305-253-2244

Balboa Life & Casualty
3349 Michelson Dr.
Irvine, CA 92715
Phone: 800-854-6115

Cardholder Brokerage Services
550 Mamaroneck Ave.
Harrison, NY 10528
Phone: 914-381-5353

CardMember Publishing Corp.
655 Washington Blvd., Suite 806
Stamford, CT 06901
Phone: 203-324-7635

CardShare Services
10825 Farnum Dr.
Omaha, NE 68154
Phone: 402-392-5575

Comp-U-Card International
707 Summer St.
Stamford, CT 06902
Phone: 203-324-9261

Cooper Rand Corporation
45 West 25th St.
New York, NY 10010
Phone: 212-463-9090

Credit Card Sentinel, Inc.
9040 Topanga Canyon Blvd.
Canoga Park, CA 91304
Phone: 818-882-9947

Credit Card Service Corp.
6860 Commercial Dr.
Springfield, VA 22151-4208
Phone: 703-658-6369

Credit Services of America
1479 Rt. 23 South
Wayne, NJ 07470
Phone: 201-628-0180

General Vitamin Corp.
P.O. Box 1500
Chapel Hill, NC 27515
Phone: 919-929-2183

Heartland Promotions
5023 Grover St.
Omaha, NE 68106
Phone: 402-558-3308

Heartland Promotions, Inc.
401 N. 117th St.
Omaha, NE 68154
Phone: 402-330-3233

Insurance Consultants, Inc.
200 Blackstone Center
Omaha, NE 68131
Phone: 800-662-8855

Insurance Specialists, Inc.
3885 Upham St.
Wheat Ridge, CO 80033
Phone: 800-445-4065

JC Penney Life Insurance Co.
2700 W. Plano Pkwy.
Plano, TX 75075
Phone: 214-881-6775

Media Syndication Group
655 Ave. of the Americas Suite 200
New York, NY 10010
Phone: 212-924-9555

S & K Associates, Inc.
467R Main St.
Melrose, MA 02176
Phone: 617-662-0400

SafeCard Services, Inc.
3001 E. Pershing Blvd.
Cheyenne, WY 82001
Phone: 307-771-2700

The Signature Group
200 N. Martingale Rd.
Schaumburg, IL 60173-2096
Phone: 708-605-3000

Telecredit Marketing Services
5301 W. Idlewild Ave.
Tampa, FL 33634
Phone: 800-237-2997

United Bank Services
2500 S. McGee
Norman, OK 73072
Phone: 800-654-3236

CARD MFG. AND SERVICES

American Plastic Card Co. Int.
21550 Oxnard St., 3rd Floor
Woodland Hills, CA 91367
Phone: 818-784-4224

Arthur Blank & Company
225 Rivermoor St.
Boston, MA 02132
Phone: 617-325-9600

Cardpro Services
135 W. 61st St.
Westmont, IL 60559-2617
Phone: 708-960-5640

Cardtech, Inc.
2020 Enterprise Pkwy.
Twinsburg, OH 44087
Phone: 216-425-1515

Caulastics, Inc.
5955 Mission St.
Daly City, CA 94014
Phone: 415-585-9600

Colorado Plasticard, Inc.
830 Kipling St.
Denver, CO 80215-5867
Phone: 303-233-8710

Continental Plastic Card Co.
3651 N.W. 120 Ave.
Coral Springs, FL 33065
Phone: 305-753-0670

Credit Card Systems, Inc.
180 Shepard Ave.
Wheeling, IL 60090
Phone: 708-459-8349

DataCard Corp.
11111 Bren Rd. West
Minneapolis, MN 55440
Phone: 612-933-1223

Data-Pro Automated Card Serv.
8904 Bash St., Suite M
Indianapolis, IN 46250
Phone: 317-579-6400

Delux Plastic Card Co.
202 S. 22nd St., Suite 102
Tampa, FL 33605
Phone: 813-248-2196

Didier Printing
613 High St.
Fort Wayne, IN 46853
Phone: 219-424-4920

Drexler Technology Corp.
2644 Bayshore Pkwy.
Mountain View, CA 94043
Phone: 415-969-7277

Faraday National Corp.
4250 Pleasant Valley Rd.
Chantilly, VA 22021
Phone: 703-263-0100

Florida Information Services
401 South Magnolia Ave.
Orlando, FL 32802
Phone: 407-841-1712

Heinrich Marketing, Inc.
830 Kipling St.
Denver, CO 80215-5867
Phone: 303-233-8660

International Plastic Cards
366 Coral Circle
El Segundo, CA 90245-4631
Phone: 213-322-4472

Kirk Plastic Company
2811 E. Ana St.
Rancho Dominguez, CA 90221
Phone: 310-884-7900

Logicard Systems, Inc.
P.O. Box 637
Armonk, NY 10504
Phone: 914-273-8734

Malco Plastics
9800 Reistertown Rd.
Owings Mills, MD 2117-4145
Phone: 410-363-1600
　　　　　800-825-1155

McCorquodale
Oaklands Corporate Center
523 James Hance Ct.
Exton, PA 19341
Phone: 215-524-2410

Micro Card Technologies, Inc.
14070 Proton Rd.
Dallas, TX 75244
Phone: 214-788-4055

National Business Systems
800 Montrose Ave.
South Plainfield, NJ 07080
Phone: 908-668-0999

Perfect Plastic Printing Corp.
345 Kautz Road
St. Charles, IL 60174
Phone: 708-584-1600

Philco Plastics
403 Calendar Rd.
Vidalia, GA 30474
Phone: 912-537-7442

Plastic Graphic Co.
484 Wegner Rd.
McHenry, IL 60050
Phone: 815-344-2240

Q-Card, Inc.
2 Chellis Ct.
Owings Mills, MC 21117
Phone: 301-581-0112

S & K Associates
467R Main St.
Melrose, MA 02176
Phone: 617-662-0400

Schlumberger Technologies
825 B. Greenbrier Circle
Chesapeake, VA 23320
Phone: 804-523-2160

Shoreline Business Forms
101 N. Plains Industrial Rd.
Wallingford, CT 06492
Phone: 203-265-9559

Sillcocks Plastics International
310 Snyder Ave.
Berkeley Heights, NJ 07922
Phone: 201-665-0300

Standard Register
P.O. Box 1167
Dayton, OH 45401
Phone: 513-443-1000

2B Systems Corporation
6575 Arrow Dr.
Sterling Heights, MI 48314
Phone: 313-254-6900

Ultra Plastic Printing, Inc.
12955 York Delta Dr., Suite N
Cleveland, OH 44133
Phone: 800-777-8080

Unique Embossing Services
1201 Butterfield Rd.
Downers Grove, IL 60515
Phone: 708-960-3337

CASSETTE TAPES

A & S Audio
5424 Henderson Rd.
Hamptonville, NC 27020
Phone: 800-472-3927

CHECK GUARANTEE AND VERIFICATION

CSA
1479 Rt. 23
Wayne, NJ 07474
Phone: 201-628-0180

Electronic Transaction Corp.
11000 Lake City Way NE
Seattle, WA 98125
Phone: 206-365-6711

TeleCheck
330 N. Brano, Suite 570
Glendale, CA
Phone: 818-243-6969

TeleCheck
3025 S. Parker Rd.
Aurora, CO 80014
Phone: 303-752-5305

COLLECTION AGENCIES

Accounts Receivable Options Inc.
11040 Holmes Rd.
Kansas City, MO 64131
Phone: 816-941-7002

A. M. Miller & Assoc.
3033 Excelsior Blvd.
Minneapolis, MN 55416
Phone: 612-928-2000

Allied Bond & Coll. Agency
One Allied Dr.
Trevose, PA 19053
Phone: 215-639-2100

American Creditors Bureau
714 E. Van Buren St.
Phoenix, AZ 85006
Phone: 602-379-2222

Bankruptcy Recovery Network
1547 W. Struck, Suite D
Orange, CA 92667
Phone: 714-771-7534

Capital Credit Corp.
492 Rt. 46 East
Fairfield, NJ 07004
Phone: 201-227-4825

CBC Companies
250 E. Town St.
Columbus, OH 43215
Phone: 614-222-4343

Coldata, Inc.
500 Rockaway Ave.
Valley Stream, NY 11581
Phone: 516-561-6644

Credit Claims & Collections
2253 Northwest Pkwy.
Atlanta, GA 30339
Phone: 404-916-5211

Credit Convertors, Inc.
260 E. Wentworth Ave.
St. Paul, MN 55118
Phone: 612-450-3000

Creditors Bankruptcy Serv.
9441 LBJ Freeway, Suite 605
Dallas, TX 75243
Phone: 214-644-1127

Credit Services of America
1479 Rt. 23 South
Wayne, NJ 07474-0978
Phone: 201-628-0180

CSC Credit Services
652 N. Belt East
Houston, TX 77060
Phone: 713-878-1900

East Coast Credit
168 Franklin Corner Rd.
Lawrenceville, NJ 08648
Phone: 609-896-8484

Equifax Accts. Rec. Services
1600 Peachtree St. NW
Atlanta, GA 30309
Phone: 404-885-8771

Financial Collection Agencies
80 W. Lancaster Ave.
Suite 400
Devon, PA 19333
Phone: 215-687-4601

FM Services Corp.
1085 N. Black Canyon Frwy.,
   Suite 850
Phoenix, AZ 85029
Phone: 602-943-0775

GC Services
6330 Gulfton St.
Houston, TX 77081
Phone: 713-777-4441

Great Lakes Coll. Bureau
625 Delaware Ave.
Buffalo, NY 14202
Phone: 716-881-6767

IC System, Inc.
444 E. Hwy. 96
St. Paul, MN 55164-0444
Phone: 612-483-8201

Integratec, Inc.
Atlanta Financial Center
East Tower, Suite 1100
333 Peachtree Rd. NE
Atlanta, GA 30326
Phone: 404-266-0522

International Credit Services
6525 Angola Rd.
Holland, OH 43528
Phone: 419-867-1671

The Master Collectors
Plaza 400
5883 Glenridge Dr., Suite 200
Atlanta, GA 30328
Phone: 404-843-9400

National Finance Systems
371 Merrick Rd.
Rockville Centre, NY 11570
Phone: 516-536-1500

National Revenue Corp.
2323 Lake Club Dr.
Columbus, OH 43232
Phone: 614-864-3377

Nationwide Collection Agencies
3302 W. St. Joseph, Suite One
Lansing, MI 48917
Phone: 517-487-1300

Payco American Corp.
180 N. Executive Dr.
Brookfield, WI 53005
Phone: 414-784-9035

Penncro Assoc., Inc.
95 James Way, Suite 113
South Hampton, PA 18966
Phone: 215-322-2438

Sunrise Credit Services
69 Merrick Rd.
Coplague, NY 11726
Phone: 516-842-8000

Transworld Systems, Inc.
5880 Commerce Blvd.
Rohnert Park, CA 94928
Phone: 707-584-4225

TRW Rec. Mgmt. Services
12606 Greenville Ave.
Dallas, TX 75243
Phone: 800-962-9876

United Recovery Systems
3100 S. Gessner, No. 400
Houston, TX 77063
Phone: 713-977-1234

Viking Collection Serv.
11095 Viking Dr.
Minneapolis, MN 55459
Phone: 612-944-7575

O. D. Young & Assoc.
9113 Woodville
Pleasant Plain, OH 45162
Phone: 513-877-2766

COLLEGE CREDIT CARD PROGRAMS

CAC Direct
1940 W. Palatine
Inverness, FL 60067
Phone: 708-359-0010

College Credit Card Corp.
1500 Walnut St., 19th Floor
Philadelphia, PA 19102

On Campus Marketing
1981 Old Cuthbert Rd.
Cherry Hill, NJ 08034
Phone: 609-795-8525

COMPUTER MFG.

CAP Industries
600 Ansin Blvd.
Hallandale, FL 33009
Phone: 305-458-4700

Concurrent Computer Corp.
106 Apple St.
Tinton Falls, NJ 07724
Phone: 908-758-7000

Data General Corp.
3400 Computer Dr.
Westboro, MA 01580
Phone: 508-898-4194

Digital Equipment Corp.
146 Main St.
Maynard, MA 01754-2571
Phone: 508-493-5111

Hewlett-Packard
3000 Hanover
Palo Alto, CA 94304
Phone: 415-857-1501

Hypercom, Inc.
2851 W. Kathleen Rd.
Phoenix, AZ 85023
Phone: 602-866-5399

IBM Corp.
1001 W. T. Harris Blvd. West
Charlotte, NC 28256
Phone: 704-595-6363

ISC-Bunker Ramo
P.O. Box TAF-C8
Spokane, WA 99220
Phone: 509-927-5600

NCR Corp.
1700 S. Patterson Blvd.
Dayton, OH 45479
Phone: 513-445-5000

Siemens Nixdorf Computer
200 Wheeler Rd.
Burlington, MA 01803
Phone: 617-273-0480

Stratus Computer, Inc.
55 Fairbanks Blvd.
Marlboro, MA 01752
Phone: 508-460-2000

Support Systems Int.
150 S. Second St.
Richmond, CA 94804
Phone: 415-234-9090

Tandem Computers, Inc.
19333 Vallco Pkwy.
Cupertino, CA 95014
Phone: 408-725-6000

Unisys Corp.
P.O. Box 500
Blue Bell, PA 19424
Phone: 215-986-3290

Wang Laboratories
1 Industrial Ave.
Lowell, MA 01851
Phone: 508-459-5000

CONSULTANTS

A & S Consulting
5424 Henderson Rd.
Hamptonville, NC 27020
Phone: 800-472-3927

Dave Abright
8035 E. R.L. Thornton, Suite 410
Dallas, TX 75228
Phone: 214-320-7867

Ferrante Financial Services
1700 Surveyor Ave.
Simi Valley, CA 93097
Phone: 805-520-8063

CONTROLLERS AND CONCENTRATORS

Hypercom, Inc.
2851 W. Kathleen Rd.
Phoenix, AZ 85023
Phone: 602-866-5399

NCR Corp.
1700 S. Patterson Blvd.
Dayton, OH 45479
Phone: 513-445-5000

Network Controls Int.
9 Woodlawn Green, Suite 120
Charlotte, NC 28217
Phone: 704-527-4357

Perle Systems, Inc.
630 Oakmont Ln.
Westmont, IL 60559
Phone: 708-789-3171

Siemens Nixdorf Info. Sys.
200 Wheeler Rd.
Burlington, MA 01803
Phone: 617-273-0480

Specialty Retail Systems
1013 S. Claremont St., Suite 5
San Mateo, CA 94402
Phone: 415-573-5665

Unisys Corp.
One Unisys Pl.
Detroit, MI 48232
Phone: 313-972-7000

Wang Laboratories
One Industrial Ave.
Lowell, MA 01851
Phone: 508-459-5000

CREDIT BUREAUS

Equifax Credit Info. Serv.
CBI
1600 Peachtree St. NW
Atlanta, GA 30302
Phone: 404-885-8000

Trans Union Credit Info. Co.
555 W. Adams St.
Chicago, IL 60661
Phone: 312-431-5100

TRW Info. Systems & Services
505 City Pkwy. West
Orange, CA 92668
Phone: 714-385-7000

CREDIT CARD PROCESSORS

Applied Card Systems
32 Reed's Way
New Castle, DE 19720
Phone: 302-322-9458

Atlantic States Bankcard Assoc.
Oberlin Rd.
Raleigh, NC 27605
Phone: 919-828-6292

Banc One Services Corp.
Bank One Center
350 S. Cleveland Ave.
Columbus, OH 43271
Phone: 614-248-4312

BT North America
2560 N. First St.
San Jose, CA 95131
Phone: 408-922-0250

Buypass, Inc.
360 Interstate N. Pkwy., Suite 400
Atlanta, GA 30339
Phone: 404-953-2664

Cardholder Mgmt. Serv.
975 Stewart Ave.
Garden City, NY 11530
Phone: 516-222-0111

CBC Companies
250 E. Town St.
Columbus, OH 43215
Phone: 614-222-5558

CFC Financial Services
535 S. Fourth St.
Louisville, KY 40202
Phone: 502-581-3033

Citicorp Establishment Serv.
2 Huntington Quadrangle
Melville, NY 11747
Phone: 800-332-0089

Computer Comm. of Am.
1235 E. Big Beaver Rd.
Troy, MI 48083
Phone: 313-828-6501

Control Data Corp.
142 W. 57th St.
New York, NY 10019
Phone: 212-887-1100

Credit Services of America
1479 Rt. 23
Wayne, NJ 07470
Phone: 800-524-0614

Credit Systems, Inc.
220 S. Jefferson Ave.
St. Louis, MO 63103
Phone: 314-231-1155

CUNA Credit Card Services
5710 Mineral Point Rd.
Madison, WI 53701
Phone: 608-231-8000

Decision Systems
251 G. Hurricane Shoals Rd.
Lawrenceville, GA 30245
Phone: 404-822-9194

EDS
18111 Preston Rd.
Dallas, TX 75252
Phone: 214-713-1300

Fast Data
2121 N. 117th Ave.
Omaha, NE 68164
Phone: 800-545-1928

Fifth Third Bank
34 Fountain Square
Cincinnati, OH 45263
Phone: 513-579-4153

First Data Retail Services
7301 Pacific St.
Omaha, NE 68114
Phone: 402-399-7000

First of Omaha
P.O. Box 3190
Omaha, NE 68103
Phone: 800-228-2443

Franklinton Financial Sys.
4661 E. Main St.
Columbus, OH 43251
Phone: 614-863-8222

G.E. Capital
1600 Summer St.
Stamford, CT 06927
Phone: 203-357-4000

General Computer Corp.
P.O. Box 364527
San Juan, PR 00936-4527
Phone: 809-751-4343

Harbridge Merchant Services
2001 Butterfield Rd.
Downers Grove, IL 60515

Household Retail Services
700 Wood Dale Rd.
Wood Dale, IL 60191
Phone: 800-333-8592

Innova Information Sys.
Five Concourse Pkwy., Suite 700
Atlanta, GA 30328
Phone: 404-396-1456

Litle & Co.
54 Stiles Rd.
Salem, NH 03079
Phone: 603-893-9333

MasterCard Automated POS
888 7th k Ave.
New York, NY 10106
Phone: 212-649-5472

Micard Services
770 N. Water St.
Milwaukee, WI 53202
Phone: 800-236-3282

NaBanco
1401 N.W. 136th Ave.
Fort Lauderdale, FL 33323
Phone: 305-785-2100

National Data Corp.
1 National Data Plaza
Atlanta, GA 30329
Phone: 404-728-2581

National Card/Ck Processing
401 S. Van Brunt St.
Englewood, NJ 07631
Phone: 201-569-7764

National City Retail Card Svc.
4661 E. Main St.
Columbus, OH 43213
Phone: 614-863-8222

National Processing Co.
1231 Durrett Ln.
Louisville, KY 40258
Phone: 502-364-2000

JC Penney Business Service
5001 Spring Valley Rd.
Suite 650, West Tower
Dallas, TX 75244
Phone: 214-591-5100

Payment Systems Co.
5200 East Lake Blvd.
Birmingham, AL 35217
Phone: 205-849-5200

PRJ, Inc.
1400 Marina Way South
Richmond, VA 94523
Phone: 510-215-5000

Rocky Mtn. BankCard Sys.
950 17th St.
Denver, CO 80202
Phone: 303-629-7755

Sears Payment Systems
2500 Lake-Cook Rd.
Riverwoods, IL 60015
Phone: 708-405-3700

SSBA America, Inc.
P.O. Box 809051
Dallas, TX 75380
Phone: 214-233-7101

T-Banc Merchant Services
120 E. Burlington Ave.
La Grange, IL 60525
Phone: 708-579-7970

Telecredit
5301 W. Idlewild Ave.
Tampa, FL 33634
Phone: 813-886-5000

Total System Services
1000 5th Ave.
Columbus, GA 31901
Phone: 404-649-2311

TransNet, Inc.
1511 N. West Shore Blvd.
Tampa, FL 33607
Phone: 813-286-8551

VisaNet POS Services
P.O. Box 8999
San Francisco, CA 94128
Phone: 415-570-3200

CREDIT MANAGEMENT SOFTWARE

Credit Card Software Group
900 Winderley Place
Maitland, FL 32751
Phone: 407-660-0343

MicroBilt
6190 Powers Ferry Rd., Suite 400
Atlanta, GA 30339
Phone: 404-955-0313

Rothenberg Computer Systems
2975 Scott Blvd.
Santa Clara, CA 95054
Phone: 408-496-6555

CREDIT SCORING SYSTEMS

American Management Sys.
1777 N. Kent St.
Arlington, VA 22209
Phone: 703-841-6404

CBC Companies
250 E. Town St.
Columbus, OH 43215
Phone: 614-222-4343

Creative Business Decisions
12 Roszel Rd., Suite A102
Princeton, NJ 08540
Phone: 609-452-9551

Credit Mgmt. Solutions
5950 Symphony Woods Rd., Suite 301
Columbia, MD 21044
Phone: 301-740-1000

Credit Partners, Inc.
1865 Palmer Ave.
Larchmont, NY 10538
Phone: 914-833-2634

Fair Isaac Co.
120 N. Redwood Dr.
San Raphael, CA 94903
Phone: 415-472-2211

Magnum Communications
1600 Parkwood Cir., Suite 300
Atlanta, GA 30339
Phone: 404-952-4940

MDS Group
945 E. Paces Ferry Rd., Suite 2600
Atlanta, GA 30326
Phone: 404-841-1400

Portfolio Mgmt. Assoc., Inc.
250 W. 57th St., Suite 1701
New York, NY 10107
Phone: 212-581-4200

Scorex
112 San Felipe Way
Novato, CA 94945
Phone: 415-899-8555

DATA PROCESSING SERVICES

Database America Companies
100 Paragon Dr.
Montvale, NJ 07645
Phone: 201-476-2000

May & Speh
1501 Opus Place
Downers Grove, IL 60515
Phone: 708-964-1501

DIRECT MAIL

Access Direct Systems
91 Executive Blvd.
Farmingdale, NY 11735-4713
Phone: 516-420-0770

Acxiom Corp.
301 Industrial Blvd.
Conway, AR 72032
Phone: 501-336-1000

Advanced Info. Marketing
2500 Westchester Ave.
Purchase, NY 10577
Phone: 914-251-0100

CAC Direct, Inc.
1940 W. Palatine
Inverness, IL 60067
Phone: 708-359-0010

Cardinal Marketing, Inc.
3340 N.W. 53rd St.
Ft. Lauderdale, FL 33309
Phone: 305-735-1900

Chandler Management Group
2021 Red Dale Dr.
Rapid City, SD 57702
Phone: 605-342-8050

Cooperative Marketing Co.
5550 Meadowbrook Dr.
Rolling Meadows, IL 60008
Phone: 708-593-3232

Coverdell & Co.
2622 Piedmont Rd. NE
Atlanta, GA 30324
Phone: 404-262-9100

CPM Research East
1491 Sheridan Rd.
Buffalo, NY 14217
Phone: 716-875-8000

Database Management
345 Park Ave. South
New York, NY 10010
Phone: 212-685-4600

Deluxe Check Printers
1080 W. County Rd. F
St. Paul, MN 55126-8201
Phone: 800-328-9584

DirectCard
6187 Grovedale Ct., Suite 100
Alexandria, VA 22310
Phone: 703-922-6888

DMDA, Inc.
1621 W. Crosby Rd.
Carrollton, TX 75006
Phone: 214-466-2611

Epsilon Financial Serv.
50 Cambridge St.
Burlington, MA 01803
Phone: 617-273-0250

First Marketing Corp.
3300 Gateway Dr.
Pompano Beach, FL 33069
Phone: 305-979-0700

Fusion Marketing Group
88 Union Ave., 6th Floor
Memphis, TN 38103
Phone: 901-526-0088

GLS Direct, Inc.
2000 Market St., Suite 1408
Philadelphia, PA 19103
Phone: 215-568-1100

Heinrich Marketing
830 Kipling St.
Denver, CO 80215-5867
Phone: 303-233-8660

Ilze C. Grace & Assoc.
30 Luzanne Circle
San Anselmo, CA 94960
Phone: 415-456-5292

Walter Latham Co.
2001 W. 21st St.
Broadview, IL 60153
Phone: 708-345-8787

Mass Mailing Service
1657 Washington St.
Holliston, MA 01746
Phone: 508-429-6741

Matrixx Marketing
1 Matrixx Plaza
Ogden, UT 84405
Phone: 800-543-6423

National Computer
5200 East Lake Blvd.
Birmingham, AL 35217
Phone: 205-849-5200

National Cr. Marketing Svcs.
7204 Harwin Dr.
Houston, TX 77036
Phone: 713-781-0262

One To One Marketing
94 East Jefryn Blvd., Suite H
Deer Park, NY 11729
Phone: 516-242-6690

JC Penney Direct
5001 Spring Valley Rd.
Suite 650, West Tower
Dallas, TX 75244
Phone: 214-960-5266

Pro Direct Response
1 Bala Plaza, Suite 222
Bala Cynwyd, PA 19004
Phone: 215-668-4100

Response Communications
933 Western Dr.
Indianapolis, IN 46241
Phone: 800-722-4724

Sungard Mailing Serv.
210 Automation Way
Birmingham, AL 35210
Phone: 205-956-7850

TABS Direct
1002 Texas Pkwy.
Stafford, TX 77477
Phone: 713-499-0417

Washburn Direct Marketing
1123 S. Church St.
Charlotte, NC 28203
Phone: 704-334-5371

FORMS AND GENERAL PRINTING

Delux Financial Forms & Supplies
2341 St. Croix St.
St. Paul, MN 55164-0497
Phone: 800-328-9600

General Credit Forms
3595 Rider Trail South
Earth City, MO 63045
Phone: 314-291-8600

Heinrich Marketing
830 Kipling St.
Denver, CO 80215-5867
Phone: 303-233-8660

Hickory Printing Group
542 Main Ave. SE
Hickory, NC 28603
Phone: 704-322-3431

Moore Business Forms
1205 Milwaukee Ave.
Glenview, IL 60025
Phone: 708-615-6000

NCR Corp.
1700 S. Patterson Blvd.
Dayton, OH 45479
Phone: 513-445-5000

PlastiCard Systems
317 W. Main St.
Apopka, FL 32712
Phone: 407-889-4120

Shoreline Business Forms
101 N. Plains Industrial Rd.
Wallingford, CT 06492
Phone: 203-265-9559

Standard Register
P.O. Box 1167
Dayton, OH 45401
Phone: 513-443-1000

Uarco, Inc.
West County Line Rd.
Barrington, IL 60010
Phone: 708-381-7000

Wallace Computer Services
4600 Roosevelt Rd.
Hillside, IL 60162
Phone: 708-449-8600

HOSTESS PROGRAMS

Bauman Group
1290 Worcester Rd.
Framingham, MA 01701
Phone: 508-879-3009

College Credit Card Corp.
210 W. Washington Sq., 11th Floor
Philadelphia, PA 19106
Phone: 215-440-9100

Greet America
8035 E. R.L. Thornton Frwy.,
    Suite 410
Dallas, TX 75228
Phone: 214-320-7867

World Class Promotions
AKA Credit Promotions
21935 Plummer St.
Chatsworth, CA 91311
Phone: 818-718-3940

MAGAZINES AND NEWSLETTERS

Card News
Phillips Publishing
7811 Montrose Rd.
Potomac, MD 20854
Phone: 301-340-2100

Credit Card Management
118 S. Clinton St., Suite 700
Chicago, IL 60661
Phone: 312-648-0261

Credit Card News
Faulkner & Gray
118 S. Clinton St., Suite 700
Chicago, IL 60661
Phone: 312-648-9569

The Nilson Report
P.O. Box 49936
Barrington Station
Los Angeles, CA 90049
Phone: 310-392-8478

MAILING LIST

Donnelley Marketing
1301 W. 22nd St.
Oak Brook, IL 60521
Phone: 312-654-2000

Metromail Corp.
360 E. 22nd St.
Lombard, IL 60148
Phone: 800-927-2238

NDL-Lifestyle Selector
1621 Eighteenth St.
Denver, CO 80202
Phone: 303-292-5000

R. L. Polk
521 Fifth Ave., 11th Floor
New York, NY 10175-0093
Phone: 212-986-0555

The Services Group
152 W. Huron St.
Chicago, IL 60610
Phone: 312-944-5094

TransMark
555 W. Adams St.
Chicago, IL 60661
Phone: 312-431-5101

TRW Marketing Services
600 City Pkwy. West, Suite 1000
Orange, CA 92668
Phone: 714-385-7766

NEW RESIDENT PROGRAMS

CPC & Associates
88 Rock Hill Rd.
Bala Cynyd, PA 19004
Phone: 215-667-1780

PREMIUMS AND INCENTIVES

Bauman Group, Inc.
1290 Worcester Rd.
Framingham, MA 01701
Phone: 508-879-3009

Greer & Associates
25354 Cypress Ave.
Hayward, CA 94544
Phone: 415-887-8711

Timco
8495 Dunwoody Place
Atlanta, GA 30350
Phone: 404-998-9805

World Class Promotions
21935 Plummer St.
Chatsworth, CA 91311
Phone: 800-572-GIFT

SERVICE BUREAUS

May & Speh
1501 Opus Place
Downers Grove, IL 60515
Phone: 708-964-1501

TELEMARKETING

Cardinal Marketing, Inc.
925 Clifton Ave.
Clifton, NJ 07013
Phone: 201-778-3766

Cooperative Marketing
5550 Meadowbrook Dr.
Rolling Meadows, IL 60008
Phone: 708-592-3232

Coverdell & Co.
2622 Piedmont Rd. NE
Atlanta, GA 30324
Phone: 404-262-9100

CPM Research East, Inc.
1495 Sheridan Rd.
Buffalo, NY 14217
Phone: 716-875-8000

DialAmerica Marketing
960 Macarthur Blvd.
Mahwah, NJ 07495
Phone: 800-531-3131

Ganett Telemarketing
6776 Southwest Frwy., No. 150
Houston, TX 77074
Phone: 713-789-9049

GLS Direct, Inc.
2000 Market St., Suite 1408
Philadelphia, PA 19103
Phone: 215-568-1100

ICT Group
800 Town Center Dr.
Langhorne, PA 19047
Phone: 215-757-0200

JC Penney Telemarketing
100 N. Corp. Dr., Suite 100
Brookfield, WI 53045
Phone: 800-323-4343

Kahn & Associates
15 Bala Ave.
Bala Cynwyd, PA 19004
Phone: 215-668-8080

Pro Direct Response
1 Bala Plaza, Suite 222
Bala Cynwyd, PA 19004
Phone: 215-668-4100

Response Communications
933 Western Dr.
Indianapolis, IN 46241
Phone: 800-722-4724

Signature Group
200 N. Martingale Rd.
Schaumburg, IL 60173-2096
Phone: 708-605-3000

Somar Telemarketing
322 East Innes St.
Salisbury, NC 28145
Phone: 704-637-6600

TeleDirect International
736 Federal St.
Davenport, IA 52083
Phone: 310-324-7720

The Telemarketing Co.
479 Business Center Dr.
Mt. Prospect, IL 60056
Phone: 708-635-1500

Wats Marketing of America
2121 N. 117th Ave.
Omaha, NE 68164
Phone: 800-351-1000

TRAVEL AND ENTERTAINMENT CARDS

AirPlus Company Ltd.
245 Hammersmith Rd.
London W67LB U.K.
Phone: 011-44-81-748-8717

American Express
American Express Tower
200 Vesey St.
New York, NY 10285
Phone: 212-640-2000

Carte Blanche
8430 W. Bryn Mawr Ave.
Chicago, IL 60631
Phone: 312-380-5160

Citicorp Diners Club
8430 W. Bryn Mawr Ave.
Chicago, IL 60631
Phone: 312-380-5160

enRoute Card International
1000 Sherbrooke St. West
Suite 2200
Montreal, Quebec H3A3G4
Phone: 514-288-1312

JCB International Cr. Cd. Ltd.
626 Wilshire Blvd., Suite 200
Los Angeles, CA 90017
Phone: 213-629-8111

TRAVEL INCENTIVE COS.

Fennell Promotions, Inc.
6640 Powers Ferry Rd., Suite 100
Atlanta, GA 30339
Phone: 404-612-0507

National Marketing Consultants
600 Morgan Falls Rd., Suite 215
Atlanta, GA 30350
Phone: 404-604-9588

Quality Services, International
4720 Boston Way
Lanham, MD 20706
Phone: 301-459-7266

UNIVERSAL CREDIT CARDS

AT&T Universal Card
8775 Baypine Rd.
Jacksonville, FL 32256
Phone: 904-443-8283

Discover Card
333 Knightsbridge Pkwy.
Lincolnshire, IL 60069
Phone: 312-634-5316

GE Rewards Card
1600 Summer St.
Stamford, CT 06927
Phone: 203-357-4728

MasterCard International
888 Seventh Ave.
New York, NY 10106
Phone: 212-649-5354

Visa USA
3125 Clearview Way
San Mateo, CA 94402
Phone: 415-570-3893

INDEX